Library of
Davidson College

European Witness

Stephen Spender

European Witness

GREENWOOD PRESS, PUBLISHERS
WESTPORT, CONNECTICUT

Copyright 1946 by Stephen Spender

All rights reserved

Originally published in 1946
by Reynal & Hitchcock, New York

Reprinted with the permission of
Harold Matson Company, Inc.

First Greenwood Reprinting 1971

Library of Congress Catalogue Card Number 74-138186

ISBN 0-8371-5643-2

Printed in the United States of America

To José

Contents

INTRODUCTION

RHINELAND JOURNEY
(July and August 1945)

1. Bad Oeynhausen	1
2. A Journey	8
3. Cologne	13
4. Conversations	17
5. Bonn	22
6. Polish Displaced Persons	25
7. A Student	29
8. Interpreter	35
9. Concentration Camp Inmate	38
10. A Day in Cologne	42
11. Nausea	55
12. Lieutenant Arran	63
13. Rudi Bach	70
14. Displaced Persons' Concert	72
15. Dinner Party	76

Contents

viii

FRENCH INTERLUDE
(May, August and October 1945)   87

JOURNEYS THROUGH THE BRITISH ZONE
(September and October 1945)

  1. An Officers' Mess   137
  2. The Film Unit   141
  3. My Driver   145
  4. Libraries   149
  5. Bonn   155
  6. Jung's Interview   161
  7. Joachim Bender   166
  8. Wuppertal   169
  9. **Goebbels**   **176**
10. Newspapers   195
11. Fire and Blood   200
12. The Student Aulach Again   206
13. Ernst Junger   211
14. Hamburg   219
15. Berlin   231

Introduction

This book is a Travel Book of a conventional kind. It is written from journals made on journeys through Germany in July and August, and again in September and October; and through France in May, August and October in 1945.

It consists of the information, the descriptions of scenery, the accounts of personalities and the general reflections which are usual in Travel Books. Any unusualness in it lies in the material itself, that is to say, in the interest, and novelty of Germany after the collapse of the Nazi regime.

I went to Germany on a mission to inquire into the lives and ideas of German intellectuals, with a particular view to discovering any surviving talent in German literature. Then later, I added to the general purpose of this mission the one of inquiring into the condition of libraries.

For various reasons the names of many of the people whom I met have been altered. In some cases, I have invented characters or incidents in order to convey some impression which could not be conveyed more directly. The book is simply a collection of impressions, with a view to building up a general picture of what I saw in Germany in 1945. It is the general picture which counts, not the isolated incidents, which, in themselves, may do less than justice to some of the people or things I saw, more than justice to others.

S. Sp.

Rhineland Journey

JULY AND AUGUST 1945

1. Bad Oeynhausen

BAD OEYNHAUSEN, IN WESTPHALIA, IS A LARGE SPRAWLING nineteenth-century health resort, full of ugly villas. The principle observed by its architects seems to have been almost to surround every villa or kursaal with a skirt and bodice of billowing trees, so that to-day the buildings flaunt their last-century modesty like middle-aged over-dressed women. You do not see the villas from a distance; you come upon them, interrupt them, surprise them round the corner. Some of them are so fantastic that one can understand their need to hide behind flounces of foliage: there are towers and domes built entirely of dark-stained pine. Then there are concert halls in the massive style of nordic granite favoured in Germany at the beginning of the present century. No road in Oeynhausen is like a road, it is self-consciously a broad path crying out to be cantered over by hooves. From these paths you get vistas of the gardens as well kempt as a short hair-cut and with flowers stuck in at strategic places like an artful coiffure.

This most German of places has now been almost completely emptied of its inhabitants and turned into the Headquarters of the Twenty-first Army Group. Everywhere Army signs are superimposed on the naïve grown-up fairy tale scenery, as though a censor had pasted his admonitions over the pictures in a children's story book. At the end of an avenue of beautiful rare trees you see notices severely asking ARE YOU ARMED? of soldiers leaving the town and going into the countryside, supposedly haunted by Werewolves. The brightly coloured wires of the Signal Corps run like stitching threads through the artificial landscape. British soldiers hurrying about in heavy boots, often carrying cutlery and mess tins, strike an anti-romantic note to this background for demoded Shepherds and Shepherdesses.

I tramped through all this scenery to find the Headquarters of Brigadier W——, an Oxford don who is a very successful soldier. He has a pale complexion, a thin face with a knife-keen expression. He told me in a friendly way that he had once heard me lecture at Queen's College, then he listened attentively while I explained that I had come to Germany to write reports on the attitude of mind of German intellectuals. He said he was interested in this, asked me to send him copies of my articles and also to come back later and tell him about my mission. He added that there had been a falling off in Intelligence Work. War-time Intelligence Officers who had been excellent had not known how to adapt themselves to peace conditions; and the lack of information about Germany to-day was almost as astonishing as had been the amount of it during the fighting. "Now that the strain of the war has gone, many Intelligence Officers don't seem to know how to get to work. I've seen displays of temperament from officers in this room during the past few weeks that they would never have shown during the war." And he continued on the same note of frankness, saying that our policy in cultural things was often mistaken. "For example, I'm protesting violently at the moment against a plan to turn the Hamburg Museum into a N.A.A.F.I. If necessary, I'm ready to throw in my commission to stop this happening. Apart from

3 Bad Oeynhausen

any other consideration, the Hamburg Museum is the only place in Germany containing ethnological evidence which makes nonsense of the Nazi racial theories."

Brigadier W—— gave me a document stating *to those whom it might concern* that I might speak freely with German civilians in pursuance of my duties (this was in the days of nonfraternization). I had hoped that after seeing him I would be able to proceed at once to Bonn. For the arrangement was that I should make a preliminary visit to Bonn and then return to London, after four weeks, to report. I had not reckoned with the difficulties of transport which kept me a further three or four days in Bad Oeynhausen. There was an arrangement by which people like myself could draw on an alleged "pool" of cars to take them on journeys. However, this pool seemed nearly always to be dry and even if a car did trickle in which one might theoretically obtain, at the last moment some person of higher priority than mine would almost certainly claim it.

There was a liaison officer, Major P——, whose function it was to press the transport claims of people like myself on the Army. P——, although a courageous officer who had been dropped in Klagenfurt during the war and used as an intermediary between us and the partisans of Yugoslavia and Austria, was perhaps too much of a poet to impress Transport Officers. He was too much of a person and not enough an official personality. He was timid, hesitant, natural, amusing and affectionate in manner, and officials are suspicious of human qualities. With his dark, rather Spanish appearance and black eyes alarmed like an animal's, it was difficult to imagine him filling in correct forms correctly.

It was irritating to hang about in Bad Oeynhausen, but the company of P—— consoled me. I had known him in Spain earlier, as he had worked for the Republicans. He told many good stories, mostly against himself.

One day P—— was sitting on a bench in the public gardens at Oeynhausen, behind a barbed-wire fence which separated the requisitioned town from some houses still occupied by civilians. On the civilian side of the fence were a small German boy and girl. The boy was eating an apple. When he had half finished it, the girl said to him: "Why don't you throw the other half of your apple to the poor British soldier, Hänschen? He looks so miserable there, sitting behind his barbed wire fence." I came to learn that there was some wisdom in this story.

In Yugoslavia, Major P—— was at one time responsible for sentencing to death, and witnessing the execution of, twelve S.S. men. These men had gone around the countryside setting fire to villages, pillaging, hanging the inhabitants on trees, etc. After he had seen them shot, P—— had the task of examining their personal belongings. Nearly all of them had left letters behind. They contained little but sentimental and romantic descriptions of scenery. "Darling Mutti, the mountains are wonderful here. You and Pappi would enjoy it." Some of these murderers and robbers had pressed flowers in albums for their sweethearts, or collected picture postcards with trite and pious inscriptions for them.

In the same way, people of France will tell you how the well-behaved apparently docile young German who showed you photographs of his wife and children, would then go out and shoot someone in cold blood or take part in burning down a village. Asked how he could combine such sentimentality with such apparent lack of feeling, he would murmur, *"Pflicht ist Pflicht,"* duty is duty. He could not relate his own personality with his actions done in the name of duty. At the same time as there was an increase in German brutality after Hitler, there was an increase in sentimentality. Other observers bear me out when I say that I have never seen even in Germany so many sentimental pictures and books and poems as are to be seen to-day in German houses requisitioned by the British and left by their owners, so many pictures of babies and butterflies and flowers, so many gleaming mountain peaks and sunsets, so many mothers and peasants and cottages and hearthsides, so many tears about home, so much commonplace about father, mother, God and beauty. All this, of course, forms only the flowers around a shrine whose image has disappeared overnight: the portraits of a heroic yet simpering, severe yet simpering, Adolf Hitler.

The atmosphere in Oeynhausen was somewhat like that of an English public school or university. Everyone seemed to go about his business with little fuss. It is difficult to believe that these soldiers, strolling about in the evenings in twos and threes, going to dances, concerts and cinemas arranged for them, were happy, but they accepted the situation with the English male cheerfulness which consists of a certain adaptability by which the Englishman seems capable at any moment in his existence of becoming a schoolboy again.

I spent four days in this depressing institutional environment. Nothing much happened and I felt as much out of Germany as everyone else must have felt, except the two or three intelligence workers associated with Major P—— in doing field work and bringing back reports about conditions in the Zone. Everything was very English. One evening I heard organ notes proceeding from an ugly red brick church well hidden behind conifers. I went in and saw in the gallery an Eighth Army officer playing Bach surrounded by a small group of other musicians waiting to play the organ in their turns. One afternoon across a square front of a building requisitioned as a barracks, I heard a soldier shouting at an A.T.S. girl: "I'd sooner sleep with a Fräulein than with one of your bloody girls anyway." At the messes most of the conversation was about "fratting." One afternoon, in the park, I sat next to a couple of the rare German inhabitants left in Bad Oeynhausen. The conversation I overheard was a proposal of marriage. The wedding having been arranged, the young couple discussed unrealistically how they would spend their honeymoon. They said they would get a Mercedes-Benz and travel. They would go to Naples. Then they would embark to South America. What was extraordinary about this conversation was that although it was only fantasy, it was without the slightest shadow of guilt. That there were material difficulties they knew, but the thought that they might not be exactly welcomed wherever they went did not disturb their dream of getting away from a Germany where everything is so uncomfortable.

In Oeynhausen I met Goronwy Rees, with whom I had once collaborated in translating Buechner's play, *Danton's Tod*. He was now a colonel. He took me to his headquarters at Luebeck, where I stayed the night. We motored through green hilly countryside which had that artificiality not of the eighteenth century but of the German fairy story. A country where the children are like dolls and where old men and women are dressed in stiff satiny peasant costume. The houses look as if you could eat them, they are all so sweet, so icing-coloured and creamful, striped with beams which look like bars of chocolate. Often they have written on them, like Happy Wishes, good thoughts charmingly lettered, painted round the outside walls under the eaves, or carved on the eaves.

These *Sprichwörter* are characteristic of German seriousness, German piety, German good intentions, German self-congratulation, the desire to label every environment with a few inches of thought sliced out of the Bible or the Poets or the Classics, the desire at the same time to reduce thought to a common denominator of banality, the desire, at the worst, of the devil to quote scripture.

The German landscape seems very German to me, because it is reflected in so many German poems and pictures, and often in the minds of the Germans. There are the great plains of the north, bare and null, interrupted by black pine forests, packed with spears and threats. There is the Nibelung landscape of waving fields with above them a jagged skyline of Tannenbaum and a threatening sky of silver shields of clouds. Then, as here in Westphalia, there is the German fairy-tale landscape; little squashed painted houses, too pretty almost to be true, and poignant deep-green fields through which homesickness seems to bleed with a dark stain of greenish blood. Germany has not the cultivated look of Italy or France, but rather a *carved* or *hewn* look; as though the curve of the hill in Westphalia, even the vineyards on the shores of the Rhine were carved and hewn, out of wood or stone, out of the landscape, instead of having grown there with the years. The little duchies and princedoms have also left many scenes resembling eighteenth-century engravings, a middle distance tinted with watery blue-greens, transparent distant hills, and in the foreground yellow-golden fields, with above a flat wall of greyish sky.

The landscape of Germany is as varied as that of any other country, yet much of it has in common a mental quality, less sensuous and luminous than France, less earthy than England. It is possible to think of it abstractly and it is possible to imagine it as full of intentions, moods. It doesn't suggest the gods and nymphs of Greece, nor is it haunted with the sense of individuals like England or France, but it is full of impulses, some warm and friendly, some sinister. It has been shaped and thought of and thought into, more than civilized. It is significant, pregnant and mystical rather than mysterious.

Goronwy Rees talked much about the Ruhr, where he had been. He described the towns as simply heaps of ruins with the people living in cellars. People stayed in the wrecks of their old homes, largely because to do so was their one chance of reuniting their families. Families were completely broken up by the war and then, since the war, by the zonal system of Occupation. The one passion of ordinary people to-day in Germany was to re-unite their families. So people stayed for months in the cellar under the remains of their old home, in the hope that Fritz, who was last heard of in East Prussia two years ago, or Lisa who had gone to Munich, would reappear.

2. A Journey

AFTER I HAD BEEN AT OEYNHAUSEN FOUR DAYS, IT SEEMED that at last my transport to Bonn had been arranged. However, when once again it was, at the last moment, cancelled, I called to mind the offer of a lift from a young officer, Captain Denton Burn, who was going to Bonn to attend the disbanding of his regiment.

I met Denton Burn at six-thirty the same evening, which was 11th July. He was a bit crestfallen (this showed on his good-looking slightly petulant public school face) and he said: "There's bad news—the car has a slow puncture." We decided to take it to the repair shop and have it pumped up well. It was useless changing to the spare tyre, because this was in an even worse condition than the punctured one, having a broken patch in the outer casing through which the inner tube bulged. When

A Journey

we got to the garage we decided that after all it would be wisest to have the tyre with the puncture not just pumped up but properly repaired. The soldier who repaired the tyre was a very talkative loose-limbed, almost albino young man, and he and Denton soon discovered that this soldier's father had been a sergeant at Aldershot when Burn had trained there. The soldier thought that old guardsmen of the last war did not understand the young Guards' soldiers of this war, and he wanted when he was demobilized to break away from home. While he told us all this, he was taking the tyre off, repairing it, and then putting it on again. When he stood with both feet on one side of the rim of the wheel and his hands levering with spanners at the tyre cover on the other side, his whole body was arched and he produced the effect of a looped caterpillar.

When he had finished with the tyre, it seemed to be set very unevenly on the wheel, in fact it bulged very much on one side. Denton Burn pointed this out, but the man said it was meant to do that and that when we had gone a hundred yards on the autobahn it would automatically have straightened out.

We set off down the autobahn, stopping occasionally to look at the tyre. It did not get straight, but we kept on thinking that it would, in another hundred yards. After we had gone twenty miles it seemed to be beginning to work itself right off the rim, so we turned round and went slowly back to Oeynhausen. After much difficulty we found the soldier again. When he took the tyre off the wheel we found that the inner tube was getting pinched. It took a long time to repair this since we had run out of rubber patches. We searched twenty lorries which were in the garage, and found only two puncture outfits both of which contained material which was rotted. I began to understand how it was that there were so many road accidents from burst tyres in Germany.

Whilst the tyre was being mended, I wandered off and had a conversation with a woman who was living in one of many prefabricated huts near the garage. She stood at the door of her hut, looked at me cadaverously, and said, "Poor Germany." I said, "Poor Holland, poor Belgium, poor Greece, poor Norway and poor Denmark." She looked at me dully again and said, "Yes, I suppose they are all badly off, but it is always poor Germany who suffers most."

It took a long time to mend the car, and after that we had supper, provided for us by the soldier in the kitchen of the barracks (luckily neither of us wore officers' badges—in fact, although I wore uniform I had no insignia of any kind). When we set out again, it was nine-thirty. After forty miles' run the tyre was completely flat. We changed it now for the tyre with the bulge. At ten-thirty, the engine went wrong, and started missing on two cylinders.

Along the side of the road we sighted a convoy of about seven large lorries. It was an R.A.F. supply convoy camping by the side of the road. We asked them to help us. Six men got to work on the engine in the dark. They had no torches (I never came across a soldier who had a torch in Germany) but they worked by the light of pools of petrol which they set on fire on the road. With the greatest cheerfulness they took most of the engine to pieces, diagnosing its ailments as they went along. They called each other by names such as Mac, Fatty, Tich and Tony-Pandy. Their conversation was full of character and humorous drama like a scene in Shakespeare, for their life was that each one should cast a role for himself of a character which fitted in with the characters of the others: that is the secret of conviviality. They lived, they said, like gipsies. They went up and down this road—Route 250—convoying supplies and camping out at night under the stars, washing in petrol and making cups of tea with water boiled in a large enamel wash-jug on the flame of a blow-lamp. Perhaps they looted a bit, perhaps later on they would "frat." But fundamentally, like all the English rank and file, they were good, because they were technicians who adored tinkering about with engines and because they did not desperately want to take away anything from anybody. They were self-sufficient, they could do without.

After two hours of hammering at it, the engine was "purring like a cat," as they pointed out. It was nearly midnight when we left them. At twelve-thirty the tyre with the bulge was flat, and the other one was still punctured. There was a wind blowing and we were on the top of an incline. It was very cold. I slept in the fields in my sleeping bag put on a ground sheet, while Denton Burn slept in the car. I was woken up at 5 A.M. by cows sniffing at me.

From five to seven-thirty we stopped every passing car, none of which could help us. At seven-thirty, Denton, carrying the two punctured tyres, got into a German civilian car and drove on to the next British convoy. I walked to a farmhouse on the other side of the road and asked if I might shave. It was a plain stone building. The farmer and his wife were friendly and gave me a glass of milk. They said they had been Nazis in the early days "when everyone was a Nazi." How indeed could simple people like themselves, they asked, "know that Hitler was going to betray us two years ago?" They said that they came from the Rhineland, where their relatives were now being terrorized by Russians, Poles and other Displaced Persons.

I left the farm and lay down in the fields not far from the car, which I felt I should watch. A good many heavy German vehicles, many of them with trailers, carrying farm workers, passed. At 11 A.M. Denton returned with his crestfallen expression. He said: "A tragedy has happened. Someone has stolen one of the wheels." After he had been put down near the convoy, which was on a side-track off the main road, he had left one wheel for exactly two minutes at the side of the autobahn, while he took the other one to the convoy. When he returned, the wheel he had left was gone. "I'm sure that one of those damned Jerry trucks must have stopped for ten seconds and whipped up my wheel."

We now only had the tyre with the inner tube (which had been repaired) bulging through the outer case. We drove slowly on to Hamm.

Hamm was the first badly damaged town I had seen. There were enormous gaps in the centre. It had lost all the appearance of having the shape of a modern town. The roads were full of people pushing hand-carts and prams to and from the station. At this time the railway stopped at Hamm, where people got out of the packed carriages and trucks to walk with their belongings on to the Ruhr towns. Women and old people held out their hands, imploring us to give them lifts. This scene of people trudging on, pushing hand-carts, carrying luggage, waiting, and imploring, all of them completely absorbed in their own acts, had the simplicity of a caricaturist's cartoon done in charcoal. The background was all broken lines and fragments, the foreground pot-holes and human misery. It was a military rule that we were not allowed to give anyone a lift.

We had much difficulty in driving through the broken streets, filled with broken people. At last we found a garage, run by an efficient sergeant, which had a depot of disused tyres and wheels collected from the wrecks of cars for miles around. The stock was so derelict, however, that it was an hour before we had found an inner tube which was not torn, rotted or badly punctured. A German workman with a boy helped with nervous eagerness, wishing to please us. The worker was an old man with a typical North German worker's face, skin drawn tight across high cheek-bones, thin flat hair brushed back over the round bony forehead, glowing furnace eyes. Denton said, rather casually I thought, "This is a German car. I requisitioned it from a Nazi." The old workman spat into the engine and said: "*Ach, die Schweine! Sie haben alle die besten Dinge gekriegt!*" (Those swine! They took the best of everything!)

We drove on to Iserlohn, where Denton left me, as he wanted to get to Bonn, and I to announce myself and my activities to the colonel in charge of that area, which included Bonn. I lunched with the Colonel and two other officers at a pleasant officers' club, a country house, built in German industrialists' country house concrete, some miles out of Iserlohn. The officers were friendly. The Colonel told me that there was indeed a reign of terror by Displaced Persons in this area, where they had murdered fifty-four persons between 15th and 25th June. The Germans were disarmed and could not resist any attacks by armed people. In the country districts all they could do was fix a large bell in the porch of each house and ring it loudly if they were attacked. But it was unlikely that anyone would come to their assistance.

3. Cologne

AT HAGEN I HAD SEEN A GOOD DEAL OF DAMAGE AND AGAIN at Hamm where most of the centre of the town was destroyed. Also all along the route from Oeynhausen there were bridges destroyed, detours, temporary wooden bridges touchingly named after some member of the "Royal Engineers"—M'-

Mahon's Bridge, Piper's Bridge, Smith's Bridge, etc.: but it was in Cologne that I realized what total destruction meant.

My first impression on passing through was of there being not a single house left. There are plenty of walls but these walls are a thin mask in front of the damp, hollow, stinking emptiness of gutted interiors. Whole streets with nothing but the walls left standing are worse than streets flattened. They are more sinister and oppressive.

Actually, there are a few habitable buildings left in Cologne; three hundred in all, I am told. One passes through street after street of houses whose windows look hollow and blackened—like the open mouth of a charred corpse; behind these windows there is nothing except floors, furniture, bits of rag, books, all dropped to the bottom of the building to form there a sodden mass.

Through the streets of Cologne thousands of people trudge all day long. These are crowds who a few years ago were shop-gazing in their city, or waiting to go to the cinema or to the opera, or stopping taxis. They are the same people who once were the ordinary inhabitants of a great city when by what now seems an unbelievable magical feat of reconstruction in time, this putrescent corpse-city was the hub of the Rhineland, with a great shopping centre, acres of plate-glass, restaurants, a massive business street containing the head offices of many banks and firms, an excellent opera, theatres, cinemas, lights in the streets at night.

Now it requires a real effort of the imagination to think back to that Cologne which I knew well ten years ago. Everything has gone. In this the destruction of Germany is quite different from even the worst that has happened in England (though not different from Poland and from parts of Russia). In England there are holes, gaps and wounds, but the surround-

Cologne

ing life of the people themselves has filled them up, creating a scar which will heal. In towns such as Cologne and those of the Ruhr, something quite different has happened. The external destruction is so great that it cannot be healed and the surrounding life of the rest of the country cannot flow into and resuscitate the city which is not only battered but also dismembered and cut off from the rest of Germany and from Europe. The ruin of the city is reflected in the internal ruin of its inhabitants who, instead of being lives that can form a scar over the city's wounds, are parasites sucking at a dead carcase, digging among the ruins for hidden food, doing business at their black market near the cathedral—the commerce of destruction instead of production.

The people who live there seem quite dissociated from Cologne. They resemble rather a tribe of wanderers who have discovered a ruined city in a desert and who are camping there, living in the cellars and hunting amongst the ruins for the booty, relics of a dead civilization.

The great city looks like a corpse and stinks like one also, with all the garbage which has not been cleared away, all the bodies still buried under heaps of stones and iron. Although the streets have been partly cleared, they still have many holes in them and some of the side streets are impassable. The general impression is that very little has been cleared away. There are landscapes of untouched ruin still left.

The Rhine with the destroyed bridges over it had a frightening grandeur on the day when I crossed over the Engineers' bridge. There were black clouds broken by glass-clear fragments of sky. Gleams of light fell on the cathedral which, being slightly damaged, looks like a worn Gothic tapestry of itself with bare patches in the roof through which one sees the canvas structure. But it is the comparatively undamaged cathedral which gives Cologne what it still retains of character. One sees that this is and was a great city, it is uplifted by the spire of the cathedral from being a mere heap of rubble and a collection of walls, like the towns of the Ruhr. Large buildings round the cathedral have been scratched and torn, and, forming a kind of cliff beneath the spires, they have a certain dignity like the cliffs and rocks under a church close to the sea.

The girders of the Rhine bridges plunged diagonally into the black waters of the Rhine frothing into swirling white around them. They looked like machines of speed diving into the river, their beautiful lines emphasizing the sense of movement. Or where they do not swoop like javelins or speedboats into the river, broken girders hang from piers in ribbons, splinters and shreds, a dance of arrested movement. In the destroyed German towns one often feels haunted by the ghost of a tremendous noise. It is impossible not to imagine the rocking explosions, the hammering of the sky upon the earth, which must have caused all this.

The effect of these corpse-towns is a grave discouragement which influences everyone living and working in Germany, the Occupying Forces as much as the German. The destruction is *serious* in more senses than one. It is a climax of deliberate effort, an achievement of our civilization, the most striking result of co-operation between nations in the twentieth century. It is the shape created by our century as the Gothic cathedral is the shape created by the Middle Ages. Everything has stopped here, that fusion of the past within the present, integrated into architecture, which forms the organic life of a city, a life quite distinct from that of the inhabitants who are, after all, only using a city as a waiting-room on their journey through time: that long, gigantic life of a city has been killed. The city is dead and the inhabitants only haunt the cellars and basements. Without their city they are rats in the cellars, or bats wheeling around the towers of the cathedral. The citizens go on existing with a base mechanical kind of life like that of insects in the crannies of walls who are too creepy and ignoble to be destroyed when the wall is torn down. The destruction of the city itself, with all its past as well as its present, is like a reproach to the people who go on living there. The sermons in the stones of Germany preach nihilism.

4. Conversations

PROFESSOR VON BECKERATH IS A VITAL, EAGER NONCONformist type with the lively, yet rather grey appearance of the teacher who regards all men who are willing to learn from him as equal.

He has a pleasant book-lined study in a house at Godesberg where he lives with his family. These houses are by no means unlike the stucco, early nineteenth-century houses of St. John's Wood in London, except that they are situated above the banks of the Rhine.

Von Beckerath was critical of the B.B.C. He said that before the capitulation everyone had been eager to hear it, but now it was boring and cautious and no one wanted to listen. The items of news from Germany were so exactly the kind which, in a country where there are almost no communications and where each part is cut off from every other part, were least interesting. To hear in Hamburg that thirty trains had gone from Cologne to Düsseldorf, or in Düsseldorf that six ships had arrived in Rostock was like hearing of events in China. What would be far more interesting—if it is impolitic to talk to Germans about Germany—would be to have at any rate a serious discussion of the situation in England, or in France, or in America. The Germans knew almost nothing about the situation of the rest of the world outside Germany. The broadcasts to Germany should therefore have a broad general political interest.

He asked: "Why cannot the B.B.C. discuss the future of Germany? Why cannot it comment on the implications of such actions as the taking over of the I.G.Farbenindustrie, actions which cause anxiety, because the I.G.F. manufacture many essential things, besides making armaments?"

I asked him what he thought of articles such as those of Franz Werfel and Thomas Mann which had appeared in the English-controlled German press. In his article, Werfel has written: "Apart from Pastor Niemöller, there was not visible amongst you one single man who honoured God more than the Gestapo."

"*Werfel wollen wir ablegen,*" "We can put Werfel aside," he answered. "He is a man who sees everything in terms of pure black or pure white, without understanding the real issues involved. Thomas Mann is, of course, more to be respected. He is a great literary artist, but as Germany's preceptor he has always cut an unhappy figure. During the last war he wrote a book in defence of Prussianism. He lacks moral authority. What we need is simple, serious men to speak to us, men whom we can respect and trust. There may be such amongst the refugees, but the whole problem of our attitude towards the refugees is very involved."

The Rector of Bonn University, Dr. Konen, is a vigorous man of seventy. He has a worn, thin, narrow face, with a refined spiritual expression. He also has a sense of humour. He likes to illustrate what he is saying with metaphor, parables, images, stories. He does not become garrulous.

Konen lives not far from Beckerath in a house on the hills of Godesberg above the Rhine, looking out over the river towards the beautiful Siebengebirge. His house is old-fashioned, crowded with furniture, but at the same time clean and bright. Konen explained the situation at Bonn University since Hitler came to power and during the war. He said that after 1933 the professors were divided among themselves into several groups. There were those who actively supported the Nazis in trying to introduce a completely nazified education into the universities; those who were active Nazis but who nevertheless retained a certain respect for objective values and for the tradition of the universities which they wished should remain independent; those who were non-active Party members; those who were not Party members but who did not oppose the Party; those who remained detached from politics; and, lastly, those who seriously tried to resist the influence of the Nazis. He said that about half the teachers in the University never supported the Nazis, and that there were never more than 45 per cent who were Party members. On the whole, he thought that a high level of teaching was maintained.

I said that most observers in England had the impression that the minds of the young were poisoned by Nazi teaching.

He said that the young were confused, spiritually starved but not poisoned in the simple and direct way that we imagined. "Try and imagine what it was like for a young person to be educated in Germany. If he became wholeheartedly a Nazi, he would be involved in endless duties and fatigues. His time would never be his own. He would be allowed no independence of thought. He would be expected to break away from all loyalties to his home and family. His parents, if they wished him to be a Nazi, would have to surrender him body and soul to the Party. In the early days a good many young people were swept completely into the Movement. But later on it was not so. During the war many of my students have visited me. I can assure you that most of them have wanted nothing more from the future than a wife, a home and a job."

As I was leaving the house, he stopped me at the door and said vigorously: "I have every confidence that if I am asked to teach my students again, I shall be able to do so. I am not frightened of the students being beyond my control. A university represents a certain benefit to the community, like a farm, and as cows provide milk, so we professors can satisfy an intellectual need."

Professor Cloos, geologist, whom I met in the classroom of an undamaged building of the University in a suburb, is a small temperamental man with untidy long hair and a sunburnt out-of-door appearance. He has a very emphatic manner. He has thrown himself into the Civil Government, organizing educational activities. He has arranged such concerts and recitals as have recently been given for civilians in Bonn.

Like the other professors whom I had visited, I deliberately selected him for interviewing because he had a reputation for being opposed to the regime. He was emphatic in his defence of his students. "The brown colour of the Nazis has spread less far than you imagine," he said. "In any case, the Rhineland is a part of Germany which has always resisted the Nazis most. I myself have always retained my influence over my pupils because they knew I was no Nazi. It was the Nazi professors who were not respected and who therefore lost their influence. Some of the students passionately desired Germany's defeat. Here in this classroom, there was a reunion of my students to toast the allied victory when the Americans landed in North Africa."

He said that several medical students evaded military service, not because they were cowards, but because they were always opposed to the war. As a geographer he was able to help a few of them to escape into Switzerland by showing them on the map the places where it was easiest to cross the frontier. He said that academic youth had always been a centre of resistance to the Nazis.

These were the statements of exceptional Germans, and they certainly do not represent the views of the ordinary German. They are the views of the few intellectuals whom Hitler always railed against because they never had faith in a German victory and they always stood outside the German community.

Even these men had certain views which, I think, show the influence of ten years of Nazi ideology. For example, they all viewed the outside world entirely in terms of power. They interpreted the Zones of allied occupation strategically. The British Zone was to them *Die Brücke*, the British bridgehead on the continent. They noted that the decision of the British that they must occupy an area of the continent from the mouth of the Rhine to the mouth of the Elbe, meant an abandonment of the former British reliance on the bridgehead of France. They did not think that we could afford ever to give up *Die Brücke*, and they therefore assumed that their fate and future was now cast together with that of Britain. They pointed out that the British, the Rhinelanders and the people of Hamburg had interests and characteristics in common, amongst which was to be counted a hatred of Prussia, and of the centralized government of Germany from Berlin. They regretted very much that we did not firmly and definitely announce our intentions with regard to Germany, so that they could envisage their future as part of the British Empire more clearly. For it was as part of the British Empire that they now were ready to see themselves, and there is nothing very striking about the question of a prominent Catholic priest, Father R—— to me: Did I believe that, in ten years, the British Zone might be granted Dominion status?

Another attitude which they shared was a bitter and unconcealed resentment and fear of the French whose occupation of part of the Rhineland they regarded as the greatest of the indignities which they had to endure. The French, they said, were beaten, they were finished as a nation and as an Empire, and the resurrection of the corpse of France by the power of the allies was intolerable to them.

Until the day of the atom bomb, they shared in common with nearly all Germans, the view that Russia would eventually either occupy the whole of the European mainland or else be defeated by the Western powers. The habit of envisaging every situation in terms of power, forced their minds to this conclusion. They pointed out that the greater part of the American army would soon have left the continent and that then the balance of power between Russia and the West would be altered decisively in favour of Russia. To the German mind, the conclusion that Russia will attack the West is inevitable.

5. Bonn

A PLEASANT ROAD, OVERSHADOWED WITH TREES, RUNNING parallel to the Rhine leads from Godesberg to the centre of Bonn which, from this end of the town, may be said to begin with the University whose entrance bridges the road. On either side of this broad leafy road there are houses and hotels, many of them destroyed. Heaps of rubble often make it impossible to keep to the pavement.

Beyond the University gate everything, including almost the whole of the main University buildings, the shopping centre and the market-place, is destroyed. Over the gate the wall of the University stood, a yellow colour, surrounded by the gleaming old statue of St. George against the sky and among the high boughs of chestnut trees. But there was nothing except charred emptiness behind this outer wall. Between the centre of the town and the Rhine everything had been smashed by shellfire in the last stages of the fighting. Occasionally I saw written on a wall some surviving Nazi slogan—VICTORY OR SIBERIA, BETTER DEATH THAN SIBERIA, WE SHALL WIN—THAT IS CERTAIN, or THE DAY OF REVENGE WILL COME. There was something strangely evangelical about these slogans and one would not have been surprised to see GOD IS LOVE or ABANDON HOPE ALL YE WHO ENTER HERE among them. Frequently there appeared on the wall a black looming figure with a question mark over his shoulder. At first I thought this might be one of the Nazi leaders or Mussolini perhaps, but it turned out to be a warning against spies.

By the banks of the Rhine, the beer gardens, hotels and great houses were all smashed to pieces. In a space amongst the ruins which formed a protected nest, there was a burnt-out German tank. Scattered all round, its ammunition lay on the ground—shells the shape of Rhine-wine bottles, still partly enclosed in their careful packings of straw and fibre.

The great bridge was down, collapsed into the river. Close to it, by a landing stage, an A.A. gun which was being used as an anti-tank gun was still pointing with terrible precision at the end of the bridge on the opposite side of the Rhine.

Bonn stank as much as Cologne or as the towns of the

Ruhr. In addition to the persistent smell which never left one alone—like an Over-Good Companion—the town was afflicted by a plague of small green midges which bred I suppose in all the rubble and also in rubbish heaps, for no rubbish had been collected for several months and in many streets there were great heaps of waste with grass and even tall potato plants growing out of a mass of grit and stalks and peel.

At night these small flies crowded thick on the walls of the bedrooms. At meals they got into any and every drink. One night I went for a walk along the banks of the Rhine. When I returned the sun had set and the flies lay like a thick bank of London pea-soup fog on either side of the river. They swarmed into my eyes, nostrils and hair, dissolving into a thick green splodge of slime when I tried to brush them off.

Every few hours during the day, Bonn was shaken by a considerable explosion. This was caused by attempts on the part of the crew of a tug in the Rhine to blow up those parts of the collapsed bridge which were obstructing river traffic.

The shops in Bonn sold practically nothing except bread and a few other rationed things. In many shops one saw various powders, which were supposed, according to their labels, to impart a pleasant ersatz flavour to food. One bookshop sold books which had apparently been dug out of rubble heaps. They were soggy with damp and they smelt like the rest of Bonn. Nevertheless, Bonn had more books than any other town in the British Zone, so far as I could discover. A few art shops sold prints and baroque statuettes.

Life seemed to have sunk in the bodies of the people to the level of the rubble in the basements and cellars of their houses. Yet certain improvements took place in conditions during the few weeks in which I was there. For example, the trams started running. The postmen started delivering postcards (letters were as yet not allowed). More trains were to be seen, and they went for longer distances. The trains were a fantastic sight. Not only did people hang on outside carriages, on the running boards, but also they clung on the buffers and crouched on the roof. Trains were covered with people as with flies.

Germans often grumbled about the Occupation, but it is only fair to add that they did not complain so much of material conditions as of mental ones. Middle-class people made incredible journeys, in crowded goods trucks, sitting on heaps of coal for days and nights, and at the end of the journey they said nothing of it. Some of the more distinguished Germans refused to take part in the German Civil Administration because they said that those who took part were benefiting by the Occupation and living better than other Germans. I have even heard of cases of the secretaries of officers, certainly not chosen for their moral qualities, refusing gifts of food for themselves and their families because they wished to show that Germans can "take it."

6. Polish Displaced Persons

SITTING ON A BENCH UNDER SOME TREES, WITH BEHIND THEM a large plain white modernist building, which has been taken over as a barracks, were six men, gazing dully out over the Rhine. They had pale blue or else brown eyes, the same salmon-pink skin like painted wood, and hair either rather weedy or else bristly.

At first I took them for members of the Reichswehr. The German soldiers now have the soulless ground-down expression as in carved-wood faces of Slav peasants. Two of the men who were older than the others looked worn and tired. They sat leaning forward, and there was a network of fine lines of painful thought on their foreheads in addition to the weathered lines around the eyes and mouths.

There was a boy, younger than the others, and a young man slightly older than he. These two younger ones in their patched blue uniforms, with their thin pinched faces, had the detached floating melancholy air of harlequins.

I asked them if they were German prisoners-of-war. They were annoyed at my asking them this, so they started talking, with the gesture of spitting at me, but with a friendliness in their resentment. They said: "No we are not German swine. We are Poles." They talked very bad German, expressing themselves with heavy gestures rather than with words. "You English are much too kind to these Germans, much too kind," one of them said. Another took up his meaning: "Now they all go round, they all go round, everyone of them, saying: 'I was never a Nazi. Oh no, I was never a Nazi.' " A third went on: "They take off their hats, they all bow. They can't be kind enough, they can't do enough for you." "They fall over themselves trying to help you."

As each spoke, he moved with angular gestures, and imitated with a tone of voice that did not really attempt to act properly, the voices of the Germans. The whole effect was of a cubist picture: these peasants with their elbowing movements, their dull voices rising to an apex of momentary irony and then sinking back again into boredom.

After a burst of speech they were silent, as though at the end of a stanza of their chorus of commentary with which they wished to provide me, a stranger, coming from an island. Then they were inspired again:

"How do you think they treated us before?" the youngest

but one asked. The chorus went on, passing from one to another. "We were herded together like cattle." "We were made to work like slaves." "Nothing was bad enough for us." "When we arrived at a place, the children used to gather round us and shout 'Dirty Polack!' 'Filthy Polack!' " There was something particularly distressing in the bitter way they said "Polack," which, in English has an affectionate ring.

"We never received a kind word from anyone, not one kind word, not a single kind word in five years." "No one ever helped us, no one ever smiled at us in a friendly way. No one." "And now they all lie to you. They say that they never liked the Nazis and that they were wanting you to come and rescue them."

The silence into which they relapsed became like a shrug of contempt. I asked: "Where did you come from?"

The oldest one, not answering my question directly, said: "Thirty thousand people were murdered in the town which we came from. The town was burned down and many people we knew were hanged on trees. But my son here escaped with me."

His son was the youngest of them, and being mentioned he looked self-conscious in a very physical way, squaring out his elbows.

"I am with my father," he said, "but we know nothing of my mother and my sister. All the others here have lost their relatives."

They all assented to this, then there was another silence, pause at the end of a stanza.

"We were paid twenty marks a month for our work. But most of even that they took away."

"Why was it taken away?" I asked.

They laughed. "Look. Two of us were made to unload a

truck of wood or coal. We were expected to do it in one morning, and at the same time we were not properly fed." "If we couldn't unload it, then we were fined a proportion of our wages." "In that way, by the end of the month, almost all our wages had been taken from us by fines." "So we were in every sense slaves."

"But now, do you want to go back to Poland?"

"Yes. We want to go back. It is our own land."

"What do you think about the Russians in your country?"

"We are not afraid of the Russians. The only people we hate are these Germans."

"We would sooner work for twenty years under the British or the Americans than for one year under the Germans."

"How would you yourselves treat the Germans?"

"We would treat them as they have treated us." "Make them work. You never make them work, as they understand how to make other people work. You're too kind to them." "You take trouble about feeding them, you calculate the rations they should have, as though they were being cared for in a hospital." "Do you think they measured out our rations?"

"Agreed that the Germans deserve whatever they get, however bad it is. But if Germany was treated as Poland has been, then the greater part of Europe would become a desert."

"Yes, that is so," they replied without interest, and they relapsed into the apathetic silence in which I had first found them.

Yet apathy is only a surface expression. Behind it there is something much more menacing, something which has happened and left its impression, the fires which burned the cities of Europe still smouldering in the minds of men. This is a state of mind which glows beyond despair, beyond the destruction of our civilization.

A Student

I have seen this expression in the faces of the desperate young men of the demobilized Reichswehr, also in those of the French repatriated prisoners and in those of other men and women labelled Displaced Persons.

7. A Student

ONE AFTERNOON AS I WAS LOOKING AT THE ROWS OF SOGGY books in a suffocating bookshop, I noticed standing beside me a young man with a freckled complexion, eyes piercing and rather close together, a sharply tipped nose which looked rather pinched as a result of his general extreme thinness. He was nicely dressed in a loose neat tweed suit of a dark colour with a jacket like a "Norfolk" jacket. He wore a very clean white shirt and a spotted bow tie. A bow tie always seeks reflections of its wings in the appearance of the wearer and Haecker's (for that was his name) tie found itself reflected in the two wings of his hair loosely brushed back and parted in the middle.

Obviously this was a student, so I asked him what he was. He said that he had been a student of law at Bonn for two years until the end of the war. Previously he had been in the Reichswehr but he had been demobilized on account of general debility, after a serious operation for appendicitis. He was also an artist and a writer, he said. He was very friendly and obviously took the kind of pleasure in talking to me that some schoolboys take in talking to prefects. He invited me back to his room, where he said he would show me some of his poems and pictures.

While we were walking through the dusty, stenching, half-ruined streets, he explained to me that his more ambitious paintings could not be seen, as they had been evacuated to the country, where, he feared, they might have been destroyed. He went on to describe his life as a student and he said: "We even formed at the University a group of anti-Nazi students, and we had contact with the Hitler school near the Drachenfels." "How many students belonged to this movement?" "About eighty. I was one of the leaders." "What action did you take against the Nazis?" "We didn't take any practical action but we had meetings in which we decided that we should interpret events and books objectively and that we should not allow our judgment to be influenced by Nazi propaganda." "Did you protest against any of the actions of the Nazi Party?" "No." "Did you resign from the Nazi Party?" "No. In order to cover activities, we all made a point of remaining Nazi Party Members. However, we each wore a small ribbon concealed within the top of the trousers, as the insignia of our movement."

He showed me this small ribbon—a typical student's device —attached to a braces' button at the top of his trousers and concealed under the jacket.

His room was on the top storey of a house which had not been destroyed. He had three or four shelves of books, some of them old Law books of the sixteenth century, beautifully printed on paper which had not faded in four hundred years.

His drawings and water colours were of a kind which Hitler would have approved. Carefully drawn studies of architectural subjects, such as cloisters or farmyards, with every stone, with every straw, carefully furrowed into the paper with pencil or ink; still lifes of green jugs, red apples and orange oranges; self-portraits of Haecker looking taut and small and worried. His poems were of the same order: love poems for maidens with sun-tanned skins kissed by the wavelets of the Rhine; then a few humorous, cynical poems in which "the poet," bristling with ideals like a battleship with guns, expresses his disappointment with humanity. They were written in free verse with a certain skilful insipidity.

Haecker also showed me an essay about Red Indians which he had written during the war and which he said was a satire on the Nazis. This essay made the point that Red Indians dressed up in skins and feathers were childish. The style had a curious whining uneasiness which read strangely in a satire.

During the next days I went for three walks with Haecker, once to the Cloisters of the Nikolaskirche, once to the Poppelsdorfer Schloss and once to the Beethovenhaus, which was closed. Haecker took a great deal of pleasure in telling me how old the Cloisters were and how he came here for spiritual refreshment. They certainly have the solid tranquillity of the earliest architecture, which one associates with wells, rocks, fonts, places of coolness and freshness. Needless to say, the Cloisters and the Poppelsdorfer Schloss featured in Haecker's sketch book.

Haecker was genuine in his love of architecture, books and beautiful things. Nevertheless, this love of his was a feeble aspect of his own weak personality. With his spruce tie, his prim look of cautious self-esteem, his combination of ingenuousness with disingenuousness, his preened pride and "humour," his whole array of little qualities all on show, he reminded me of a pre-Raphaelite painting I have seen in the London Tate Gallery of Isabella from Keats's *Isabella and the Pot of Basil*. Isabella is depicted as a spruce yet dejected maiden bending down to water the pot of basil, which reminded me of the little array of poor Haecker's qualities.

He was very anxious to please. He gave me two small eighteenth-century engravings of the University of Bonn at the time when it was a ducal palace. Haecker was not the only young German who showed me an almost oriental courtesy.

One day I saw another student walking down the road reading on a single sheet of paper a very beautifully printed (as I thought) poem. The style of the lettering made me think the poem might be by Stefan George, so I spoke to the student. He explained to me that the poem was not printed but written by himself in a calligraphy which one truly could not distinguish from printing. It was a masterpiece of misapplied craft. Seeing that I was interested he immediately pressed me to accept this poem, which must have taken him hours to inscribe.

Such acts of generosity amaze and often infuriate the soldiers now occupying Germany who have wasted years fighting an intractable enemy who receives them not with bullets, but with *billets doux*. They are interpreted as showing the ingratiating insincerity of the German character. Yet I do not think that this criticism is entirely just. Often, as with Haecker, ingratiating behaviour is combined with a certain pride, and I think it is the adolescence rather than the servility of Germans which makes them incline first to knock you down and then be friends.

When he was not presenting himself to me (and also to himself) as a conventionalized cultivated student, Haecker often made remarks which were surprisingly and doubly revealing. Doubly revealing, because in themselves they were revealing, and because the very fact that he said them revealed how, although he was always trying to impress me favourably, he had absolutely no idea that what he was saying would surprise me. That he often told me exactly what he thought, showed his complete ignorance of the ideas in my mind.

Haecker described himself and the fellow-students who claimed to be anti-Nazis, as not Nazi but "Nationalist." "Of course, Hitler's anti-Semitism was a great mistake. The Jews were an almost harmless, insignificant, inferior section of the population, and it was absurd to persecute them, especially as the fact that they were persecuted united foreign opinion abroad against Germany. All the same, though, race is real. We Germans really do belong to a Nordic stock which is different from and superior to the Southern and, especially, the Eastern peoples. The great mistake of the Nazis was to have obscured and distorted the true racial issue (I mean, of the West against the East) by introducing it as the Jewish problem. If the Nazis had not done this, then the English and the Americans would have fought with us against the Japanese. Also we would have supported the British Empire against the East in India."

"But how can you believe that a Nordic race which—even if they include amongst them the British and the Americans—nevertheless also include a people who produce a Buchenwald and a Belsen: how can you believe that such a Nordic race can be superior to the East?" I asked.

"I don't believe that the events which we have been told of actually happened at Belsen and Buchenwald."

"Why not? Haven't you read about them?"

"Of course, I have studied the whole question very closely," he said, with a little *moue* of self-esteem on his fastidious mouth, "but I don't believe these things happened, not even under the Nazis." He referred to the Nazis as to a mythical race which had passed altogether off the face of the earth.

"Why not?"

"Because the things which I have read about are humanly impossible." (*Menschlich unmöglich* was his phrase.)

"I can assure you that they did take place and, if you don't believe it, I shall try to take steps to provide you with the proofs."

He was seated, half-reclining during this conversation on

a divan. When I spoke of providing him with proof he recoiled as though I had threatened to strike him. Then he said quickly: "If you tell me it is so, of course I believe you." This did not sound sincere, but I dropped the matter.

On the afternoon in which we walked through the pleasant gardens of the Poppelsdorfer Schloss, Haecker talked of literature. He assured me that "we young people" didn't attach any importance to Thomas Mann, who produced works of "pure literary value." He assured me that there were many good "young writers," but he could not name them. He seemed to take it for granted that every year there were young writers as there are spring lambs. He observed a disdain towards the entire past, and he combined a complete conventionality and unoriginality of outlook, with a sense of his being a representative of a superior new generation.

When we left Poppelsdorf we walked along a badly bombed avenue which leads from the palace to the next town. "This is where the Edelweiss movement carried out some of its attacks," he said. "Who were they?" I asked. He explained that in the last stages of the war there was a sporadic movement of youths and children who carried out acts of pure destruction and who often waylaid and robbed people. These outbreaks were given a strange unity, by the fact that children charged with acts of hooliganism in widely separated parts of Germany, at a time when communications had so largely broken down, explained that they were members of the Edelweiss movement.

As we walked back to the Transit Mess, through the Market Square, Haecker asked me whether the German Secret Weapons, V_1 and V_2, had done much damage to England. I said that they were most unpleasant and that they had done a great deal of damage, though they were inaccurate. Haecker exclaimed: "Oh, I never believed they had done any damage!

35   Interpreter

At that stage of the war, I took it for granted that everything we read in the newspapers was propaganda and that one could not believe a word of it." I wondered how his morale would have been if he had believed the stories of damage done by V1 and V2.

8. Interpreter

A BRITISH OFFICER AT THE MESS SUGGESTED THAT I SHOULD interview his interpreter whom he described as "an exceptionally sincere and intelligent fellow." So a few days later a heavy elderly man with pouches of flesh hanging round his jaws, not quite horizontal eyes sloping groundwards from the bridge of his nose and a bald head, came into my room. He bowed and smirked with the exaggerated respect shown by many members of the Master Race to their Occupiers. Then he sat awkwardly at the edge of a chair, shuffling his feet. He accepted a cigarette with a bow of Oriental abasement over my fingers as I offered it to him, and then the conversation began.

He explained that he was a translator of Shakespeare, better than all previous translators. I said I was surprised to hear this as I had heard it claimed that translations of Shakespeare into German were so good that many Germans considered Shakespeare to be better in German than in English. "Yes," he said, very clearly and distinctly, holding up a finger to emphasize each point, and not so much catching as entangling my eyes in his own watchful drooping bloodhound gaze, "but the other translators have omitted from their work the Shakespearean Harmony. In my version I have restored the Shakespearean Harmony to the German langauge. For example, take the speech 'To be or not to be,' *'sein oder nicht sein.'* After several lines there comes the line 'To sleep, to die, no more.' All the other translators have rendered this:

Schlafen, sterben, nichts weiter.

But I have translated it as:

Schlafen, sterben, sonst nichts,

which is nearer the original rhythm of

To sleep, to die, no more.

Thus I have introduced into the German the original rhythm of the English."

"Have your translations been produced in Germany?"

"During recent years, yes, but not earlier, because there were Forces which prevented their being produced."

"What Forces?"

"For me to explain that, you must first understand the position of culture in Germany until the year 1933."

He then assumed an arrogant lecturing manner which was the more noticeable by contrast with the almost cringing way in which he had entered the room.

Up to 1933, he now explained, the whole of German culture—particularly the films, theatre and music—had been under the control of the Jews, and, in the Rhineland particularly, also those of the Catholics. No one could produce, conduct, act, perform, publish, who was not approved by the Jews. Orchestras were run by Jews, films were made by Jews, critics were Jews. Then, he continued—with the assurance and pious simplicity of one telling a Bible story to a child—a great movement arose, a Movement of Faith—a *Glaubensbewegung.* The aim of this movement was to unite the Christians who were Germans and conscious of being Germans, against the Jews, on the one hand,

and, on the other, against the Princes of the Church who recognized a loyalty to Rome before that of their duty towards Germany.

I asked him whether he was referring to Reichsbishop Mueller's German Christians. He looked somewhat embarrassed and replied: "Not entirely, but perhaps, more or less." Then he went on with his Bible story, by-passing, as it were, my interruption.

"There was an unjust agitation against this movement of Christian unity, and naturally some of the discordant agitators, who wanted to undermine German unity with foreign loyalties, had to be set aside."

"What do you mean by 'set aside'?"

"Naturally, some Jews and Catholics had to be put away, locked up, because they sought to destroy the unity of the German *Glaubensbewegung*."

"When you say so mildly that they had to be set aside, are you aware of what they really had to endure?"

"Naturally, I have read what we have been told in the newspapers about Belsen and Buchenwald. I know nothing about all that, of course."

"Of course?"

"Now that I have read these things, I don't understand how they could have happened. I am quite sure that the Führer knew nothing about what was going on. Maybe there were people around him"—he shifted from haunch to haunch uncomfortably—"Himmler, perhaps, or Goering, who were responsible. My impression is that the Führer knew nothing. In the first years, when the movement was full of idealism and good acts, he was in control. Then the others who were round him cheated him, and hid things from him more and more."

"Were you a member of the Nazi Party?"

European Witness

The interpreter drew himself up proudly: "As an intellectual, a translator, a man of letters and an artist," he said, "I have been always independent of Party. I could not allow my Mind to be identified with the ideas of any political movement."

Later, I told the officer who had sent this man to me that his interpreter was one of the most outspoken Nazis I had met since 1933 though not a member of the Party. He was rather surprised, but not really at all shaken in his conviction that he was fortunate in having a remarkably intelligent interpreter, a man full of ideas.

9. Concentration Camp Inmate

ONE AFTERNOON WHILE I WAS WALKING ALONG THE ROAD which goes alongside the railway from Bonn to Godesberg, a young man came up to me and asked if I would stop a car and request the driver to take him to Godesberg. While we were standing by the side of the road waiting for the car, I thought that perhaps I should see his papers, so I asked him to show me them. He showed me a paper, signed by the Commanding Officer of Bonn, to say that he was Rudolf Clarens who had spent six years in the Concentration Camp of Esterwegen. This paper asked the *Office for Those Who had Suffered Injuries Through Fascist Oppression* to render him assistance in the form of money and clothing.

Clarens was unshaved and dressed in extremely dirty clothes with a shirt torn open and revealing his thin white chest. He had a square bony head covered with short dark brown hair, and eyes with a rather fixed gaze, each of a slightly different brown colour which made them appear to have different expressions. His face had a look of silence and suppressed eagerness, like the faces of some blind beggars and also like the faces of some of the unemployed during the great slump of 1931. He smiled timidly at me with a friendliness which, although it was not uncalculating, was different from the subservience of the translator or Haecker.

He said that he had been a student at Aachen. At the age of seventeen he had been arrested and sent to a concentration camp. He was now twenty-three. He wished as soon as possible to resume his studies, in order that he might become a journalist.

I asked him to call on me at the Transit Mess Hotel the following afternoon, as I was interested to know what would be the result of his visit to the office at Godesberg.

The next day he arrived at four-thirty while I was having a large tea in the lounge. I could not offer him, a German civilian, tea, so I sent him up to my room while I finished off my excellent repast with far more butter and jam than one gets in England. I was aware of the contrast between my own standard of living and that of this concentration camp inmate, but although this worried me, on the whole it had the effect of making me eat perhaps a slightly larger tea than I would have done otherwise, because this worry was a form of anxiety and anxiety tends to make me greedy.

When I went up to my room I found Clarens looking better dressed than before. He said that he had borrowed a suit from people with whom he had been staying. I noticed that both his wrists were bound round with straps. He said that this was to strengthen them because they had been weakened by digging the moor at Esterwegen. He said that the *Wohlfahrtsamt für Beschädigte* had not given him clothes but had given him thirty marks. I said that I would like to inquire into this and I left the room, announcing my intention of telephoning the *Beschädigungsamt*. I could not get on to this number, however. He did not look perturbed at my saying this; he just sat in his chair with his usual air of patiently waiting like an animal, with his hands resting on his thighs, fists slightly clenched. He looked as if he were made of light and springy wood.

By the time I came back, another visitor, Dr. L——, the University librarian, had arrived. Dr. L—— who was a pink-complexioned mild-mannered man of about fifty-five, with rather protruding pale blue eyes, was looking with pink and blue astonishment at Clarens, who, although he appeared poor and out of place, yet looked at ease to the extent that he would have looked at ease anywhere. Before, at the age of seventeen, he went to the Concentration Camp, he had been (as I got him now to explain, excusing myself to Dr. L——), in Holland. So whatever he may have done to be sent to a Concentration Camp (and he may have committed some quite ordinary crime) he had not shared the everyday experiences of every other German civilian during the past six years of the Nazi regime.

I asked Clarens what he proposed to do now. He said hitch-hike to Freiburg, where his mother lived. There he would rest for a time, after which he would write a book. What would his book be about? "My experiences in a Concentration Camp." "What will it be called?" *"Human Beasts."* "Please give me an outline of some of the incidents which are to be in it, because your experiences interest me."

At this he leaned forward in his chair, clasped his hands together, half-closed his eyes and began to recite in a low voice. What he recited began with some such phrases as: "How is it possible that human beings can behave to other human beings with an inhumanity far greater than that ever shown by the animals. . . ." By heart, he developed this thought rhetorically for some minutes. Dr. L—— opened his china blue eyes in his pink face ever wider and wider. Clarens then began speaking about the godlessness of humanity, and I realized that if ever he wrote his book, all of it would be like this and that it would contain nothing sharp, fierce, concrete or interesting.

But I was reminded by this recitation of a scene in Spain when onto the stage of a theatre where a meeting was being held, a German hero of the International Brigade was wheeled in a chair, and with the same half-closed eyes, the same swooning dead-pale expression, he spoke about the crimes of Fascism. I had then been overwhelmed and at the same time horrified, feeling that while the young German commanded all my sympathy, somewhere a serpent lurked in the heart of his romanticism.

When Clarens had finished reciting I questioned him about some of his actual experiences. He said that when he was fifteen he had left Germany and wandered about Holland. Then he had been taken up by a "Countess aged forty-five who was still a beautiful woman." Here he looked confidentially at Dr. L—— who merely looked down primly at his fine hands with their well-trimmed nails, folded neatly as kid gloves on his neat grey flannel trousers. The Countess was a socialist Countess, apparently, and she had instructed Clarens in the falsity of the Nazi ideas which had been imbued in him by the Hitler Youth organization. He had returned to Germany and taken part in anti-Nazi activities. He was probably one of those youths who have been used by political parties, often by both sides, in the great underground struggle of Left versus Right during the past decade.

He told me some curious details of his experiences when

he was arrested and examined by the Gestapo. They made him walk along a corridor which was traversed by another corridor. When he reached the place where the corridors crossed, shots were fired across his path. They put him in a cellar like a showerbath. This was constantly filled up with water which he had to pump out with a handle in order to save himself from being drowned. The strangest of his stories was that when he had been beaten and thrown into a cell one of the S.S. men, who, as he said "seemed more human than the others," came into the cell with a large ball made of wood and played a game of football with him.

When Clarens was gone I said to Dr. L——: "What did you think of that young man? Did you believe what he was saying?" "I don't know what to think," said L——. "He didn't seem to me altogether very honourable, but there were things which it is difficult not to believe. For example, I can hardly imagine he invented the story about the wooden ball."

10. A Day in Cologne

ONE MORNING I WENT FOR THE DAY TO COLOGNE. AS SOON as I arrived there, I called at once on Dr. Grosche, a clever, formerly rather modish Catholic priest, who inhabits one of the very few houses left standing in the neighbourhood of the Cathedral. It is a charming eighteenth- or seventeenth-century house built plainly in stone not unlike many a house in Bath or Wells.

Dr. Grosche was not at home so I waited for some minutes in a waiting-room which contained a Roneoing machine, stationery and parish magazines. A nun was putting leaflets into

A Day in Cologne

envelopes. There was another pious-looking woman with a face like a squashed bun, who immediately she saw me introduced herself saying: "You are an Englishman. Oh, perhaps you are sent by God to help us." I was not surprised, as I thought it extremely likely that I was sent by God for some purpose or other. "My name is Fräulein Dr. Fuhlsamer," she said, "Headmistress of the Girls' School at D——." She explained that she had a nephew called Rudi Bach who was dying of a heart disease at the civilian hospital in Bonn. She showed me certificates from a German doctor witnessing that he could only be saved by penicillin, together with a letter from an English Major saying that unfortunately supplies of penicillin were not available for the use of German civilians as we had not enough for the uses of the British. She pointed out that the Fuhlsamers were a well-known Catholic family, anti-Nazi, etc. I reflected that in any case the boy was very young, so I advised her to go immediately to Bonn and to speak there with the Town Major, a kindly and well-disposed man. I gave her a note to the Town Major. She raised her eyes to heaven and declared that I was *"Gott gesandt."* She inscribed for me a book which she had written on the Catholic Woman in Art, beginning with the Virgin Mary.

As Dr. Grosche did not appear, I went to the Town Hall and called on Dr. Adenauer, the Oberbürgermeister (Lord Mayor). He was in and expecting me, as my arrival had been telephoned by the editor of the *Koelnischer Kourier*.

Adenauer is a prominent Catholic in the Rhineland, who was Mayor of Cologne before Hitler came to power. It is now with a special personal emotion that he takes up the restoration of that Cologne which was broken like a trayload of crockery when it was taken out of his hands. When he was last Lord Mayor he was in his fifties, he is now a man of seventy. He has an energetic, though somewhat insignificant appearance: a long lean oval face, almost no hair, small blue active eyes, a little button nose and a reddish complexion. He looks remarkably young and he has the quietly confident manner of a successful and attentive young man.

His office was plain but large, situated in one of the few large office buildings left in Cologne. When I went in, he welcomed me cordially, remarking that he had heard my name before, because he had been interviewed by one of a previous generation of Spenders after the last war. It is rather curious that having retained the name Spender in his mind for over twenty years, he called me Herr Stenter during the rest of the conversation.

Talking with Adenauer when I entered the room was another man, whom he introduced to me as Professor Kroll. The editor of the *Koelnischer Kourier* had explained to Adenauer my mission, and now he said: "You could not have come at a more suitable moment because I have just appointed Professor Kroll who is here with me, to be in charge of cultural affairs— Schools, Art and Knowledge—*(Schulen, Kunst und Wissenschaft)* in Cologne.

"There are two aspects of Reconstruction which we consider of equal importance," he went on, "one, the material rebuilding of the city. But just as important is the creation of a new spiritual life. You can't have failed to notice that the Nazis have laid German culture just as flat as the ruins of the Rhineland and the Ruhr. Fifteen years of Nazi rule have left Germany a spiritual desert, and perhaps it is more necessary to draw attention to this than to the physical ruins, for the spiritual devastation is not so apparent. There is a hunger and thirst now for spiritual values in Germany. This is especially true of Cologne because here, in the past, we have had such a

A Day in Cologne

significant spiritual life and activity. Here it is to-day possible to do a great deal. Only the best should be our aim. We should have in Cologne the best education, the best books, the best newspapers, the best music."

He spoke like a man filled with a sense of civic pride for Cologne, some of whose ruins, on the other side of the square, I was looking at through the window behind his head while he spoke.

I asked him whether he thought that the young people of Cologne were poisoned by Nazi ideas.

He said that according to his own observation the young people of between fifteen and twenty-five showed an unexpected thirst for things of the spirit. Kroll nodded his head in agreement. "Our young people are like a dry sponge waiting to immerse themselves in knowledge."

Adenauer criticized the attitude which the Americans had adopted in the early days of the Occupation towards the Universities. The Americans—and also the British—had at first taken the view that the schools should only be opened for children up to the age of fourteen because the minds of those over fourteen were too perverted by Nazi doctrines for them to receive ordinary education. Adenauer said: "I think that the children up to the age of fourteen don't really matter. They can afford to hang about. The real crisis of Germany is taking place in the minds of the young people over fourteen, up to the age of twenty-five. These should be brought in contact with teachers as soon as possible." He also attached great importance to occupational training.

The point that Adenauer came back to again and again— his whole position rested on it—was that the Germans were really starving spiritually, and that it was therefore of the utmost importance to give their minds and souls some food.

He spoke of schools, of the theatre, of the cinema, of books, of concerts. He said that he would like there to be a great newspaper in Cologne which should be the counterpart in the British Zone (he seemed to think I would find this specially attractive) to the *Frankfurter Zeitung,* if that great newspaper were revived in the South. He was in contact with Holbach, the Bürgermeister of Frankfurt who said that it would be possible to start the *Frankfurter Zeitung* in October. Adenauer's idea was that the cultural side of the *Frankfurter* could, to a great extent, be reproduced in the *Koelnische Zeitung* (the former newspaper of Cologne published before the War, not to be confused with the *Koelnischer Kourier,* the news sheet edited by the Occupying Forces). Thus, each great newspaper would in a sense be a local edition of the other. Holbach, he said, was agreed to this.

He had a plan for rebuilding Cologne. This was to build a ring of satellite towns around the city and then gradually to start destroying and rebuilding the city itself. He had a scheme for producing an excellent cultural magazine immediately by printing selections of the best talks given all over the world every day on the radio. He said that he listened to many of these talks, and was surprised to find how interesting and well-informed they were. In the present situation of Germany they were a source of information which could immediately be tapped and put at the disposal of the German public without any great effort.

Our conversation ended with Adenauer saying emphatically: "The imagination has to be provided for."

After leaving Adenauer I lunched with Henry Graebner and other members of the staff of the *Koelnischer Kourier.* They lived in a house on the outskirts of Cologne. It was only slightly damaged, but they had no running water, as the water system of the town had not yet been repaired. Graebner, a Danziger by origin, with fair hair, pale blue eyes and a stocky figure, was full of vigorous, tendentious theories about how to run the German press. These editors worked in restricted, difficult conditions, but they were doing a good deal to enliven Cologne. For example, they had almost adopted the State Orchestra; and they asked me, when I returned to London, to obtain strings for the harp, which had none, and the orchestral score of one of Beethoven's piano concertos.

After lunch I called again on Dr. Grosche, who was now at home. He was a cultured, sensible priest, probably a Jesuit. He began by talking of his friends in England and France, in particular of the Bishop of Chichester and Paul Claudel. I noticed in the library—where we converged—all the books of Claudel and six volumes of André Gide, with other modern French books.

He deplored the isolation of Germany, he said that even the leaders of the Church were almost completely cut off from other leaders, outside Germany.

As he said this, I couldn't help thinking of another organized community of intellectuals in Germany which is certainly not without outside contacts: I mean the men of science. As soon as the Allies had occupied a large part of Germany they got into touch with scientists, particularly the inventors of secret weapons, many of whom were transported to England, America and Russia, where they were provided with laboratories, and where, presumably, they were living in circumstances of contact with people who share their ideas, which would be the envy of most people in Germany, the Occupying Forces as well as the Germans.

Not only were scientists taken out of Germany, but there was competition for many heads of business, especially businesses which comprised technical processes such as colour-printing, which had made great advances during the war. More recently, technicians have been sent to all the Zones for the purpose of getting in touch with German technicians and arranging such things as the removal of German machinery to other countries.

Looking at Dr. Grosche, while he explained to me that German Bishops had almost no connection with the spiritual leaders of the rest of the world, I thought that if instead of being the leaders of the Christian Churches they had been leaders in the development of some technique of material development, they would have been provided with aeroplanes to take them to conferences with their European confreres. Russia, America, Britain and France, would be competing to offer the Sees of Moscow, New York, London and Paris to some Bishop who was supposed to have made great advances during the war in Theology. In a Christian society there would be a real desire in the outer world to get in touch with the German Church leaders, because unlike the scientists, they were men who for the most part resisted Hitler and because they must have learned lessons of suffering of as great a general interest to the welfare of mankind as technical processes and secret weapons.

Yet a few weeks after my interview with Dr. Grosche, a prominent official of the Foreign Office, himself a Roman Catholic, explained to me that it was well nigh impossible to put the heads of the German Churches in touch with those of the other European Churches because Germany had made herself so hated. Another reason might be because in the modern world, religion, learning and the general interest of humanity are taken less seriously than industrial invention and business. I could not help reflecting that if the Foreign Office official had been a member of I.C.I., instead of the Catholic Church, he would not have been explaining to me that Germans were so hated that it was most difficult for German inventors to meet American or British inventors.

Dr. Grosche went on to ask me the question which all the German intellectuals ask: Could not English books and newspapers be sent to Germany? Could not the interchange of ideas between his country and the rest of the world be resumed at the earliest possible moment?

He said: "I must admit that I am disappointed with your occupation. I listened to the B.B.C. before the end of the war, and I saw your leaflets. In your propaganda—which I took to be different from that of Goebbels—you always insisted that you stood for freedom of self-expression and for discrimination between the Nazis and the anti-Nazis in Germany. Yet you have not fulfilled your promises. Of course, I didn't expect the Occupation to be anything but hard, but I did expect that you would support intellectual freedom, that you would bring an atmosphere of liberty, of idealism and of vital and new ideas to us."

Like many of the professors at Bonn, he said that he and other Roman Catholics of the older generation had never believed in or wished for a German victory, "though, at times, all the facts seemed to point to such outcome. For the Nazis to have won would have been the greatest tragedy for the Church in Germany, because total victory would have been the sign for Hitler finally to eliminate the forces opposing him. We older people were all in agreement about this. The younger ones were more divided. As Catholics they hated the Nazis, even when they had to join the Hitler youth, but despite everything they felt that they had to fight for their country."

Dr. Grosche was evidently a supporter of the Christian Democratic Party, about which I was to hear a good deal later on. He said that he did not think the Catholics should concern themselves with a return to Party Politics and a revival of the old Catholic Centre Party. They should co-operate with the Protestants in trying to promote a christian outlook. Above all, they should resist political extremism, whether from the Left or from the Right.

He explained to me his own personal opinion that all politics should be based on local politics because "voters should vote for men whom they knew they could trust, rather than for political causes." Locally-elected bodies should choose higher bodies in a pyramidal system leading up to a supreme legislative assembly. Nation-wide controversies which cut across this system of politics based on personality, could be decided by referendum.

After leaving Dr. Grosche, I went for a few minutes to see Dr. Melchers, a bookseller. The only point of interest which emerged from my conversation with him was that, working on the usual assumption of most Germans that the Zones are spheres of international rivalry between the Occupying Powers, Melchers suggested to me that the British should make Cologne into a centre of publishing and book distribution, in order to compete with the Americans who were making a centre of the book trade at Wiesbaden.

Melchers also gave me the names of a few German writers living to-day (he thought) in Germany: Friedrich Georg Jünger, the poet, brother of Ernst Jünger; Stefan Anders, a story writer; Werner Bergengruen, novelist and poet; Theodor Haecker, Catholic philosopher; Herbert Frank, translator from the Chinese, now working as a clerk in a bank at Cologne.

Later I saw some of Jünger's poems. Perhaps there are ones more interesting than those which I was shown, which had the merit of being careful and clear imitations of the manner and

A Day in Cologne

thought of Goethe's *West-Oestlicher Divan*. A friend of mine who met him in Italy tells me that Anders has written a three volume novel about the Nazi regime. Herbert Frank I met later in Cologne. He is a sensitive and intelligent scholar and he impressed me very favourably by reason of his uncomplaining and courageous attitude. But he can scarcely be described as a writer as, apart from a few translations from the Chinese and essays on Chinese culture, he has scarcely written at all.

Professor Kroll whom I had met with Adenauer in the morning had then invited me to tea. He has a pleasant house in Marienburg, a fairly undamaged suburb of Cologne. Books, a grand piano, excellent gramophone records, Piranesi engravings of Italy. All these seemed unusual in Germany to-day. This house, and glimpses of the houses in the same street, made me remember that other "New Germany" of advanced architecture and a self-consciously free and self-expressive way of life which seemed to promise so much in the nineteen-twenties. Nothing is stranger than to see in the suburbs of Cologne and on the eastern bank of the river evidences of this purposeful, novel, well-planned democratic Germany now sharing the fate of the rest of the country. The famous Exhibition Buildings, with their emphatic vertical lines which resemble a modernistic interpretation in red brick of the Houses of Parliament are now a ruin of bricks torn away from a shabby skeleton of steel.

Kroll, like Adenauer, belonged to an older type of pre-Nazi New German, in the days when the New Germany meant town-planning, sun-bathing, promising but rather amateurish developments in painting and literature, Social Democracy, the Centre Party, Psychoanalysis and all the complexes of the Weimar Republic. Kroll vaguely resembled Goethe in his old age —a somewhat dyspeptic Goethe—and, as though to remind one of the fact, there was a drawing of Goethe at exactly Kroll's own time of life on the wall of his drawing-room.

"Which of my plans do you want to hear about? I have so many plans!" Kroll said when I asked him to speak about his proposals for renewing the cultural life of Cologne.

"Which do you consider your most immediate and important task?"

"Education, undoubtedly. I agree with the Oberbürgermeister that the students are not nazified—the war cured them of that—but they know nothing, absolutely nothing. German education has never touched such a low level—except in certain technical branches—as after the Nazis came to power. You have only to look at a letter from any young German. The German youths write in a handwriting which is completely uneducated. Their autographs are those of people who have just ceased to be illiterate. They must begin right from the beginning again, learning the very simplest things, even learning to write.

"Apart from this, many young Germans haven't even received such education as the Nazis did provide. They have left school at an early age and since then have learned nothing except to make war. Many who should have gone to the university have never done so. In the schools many things which should have been taught have been omitted. There has been no history and no literature worthy of the name. Biology has been perverted.

"In spite of their abysmal ignorance, the young people show a real spiritual thirst for learning. They find themselves with a double need. They come back from the war to find perhaps that they have lost home, family, all their possessions. Then, when they ask themselves the inevitable question: 'What shall I do?', they are confronted with another question: 'What shall I think?' Then they find that they have no values, no guidance, no general culture which they can bring to bear on their situation.

"So that is the main problem, and I have a definite plan. It is that they should work with their hands as well as with their minds. My theory is based on the fact that they have been accustomed to doing hard physical labour. Therefore to start them immediately on purely mental labour would cause a disassociation in their minds between the idea of present mental and past physical tasks. They would think that mental work was the opposite of the communal efforts in which they have formerly been involved. But we want them to feel that thought and the task of physically rebuilding the new Germany are aspects of the same thing. We don't want them to be too abstract or cerebral."

"How would you make them combine physical with mental tasks?"

"I'd set them to work rebuilding the university. In the mornings they could reconstruct their own lecture rooms. In the afternoons they could have very simple lessons. I'd pay them for their work. Let them dig and let them clean up the place. Let them do very simple tasks at first, bearing in mind their complete ignorance. After a period in which they have been doing very simple work one could begin to sort them out into the bright and the dull."

Kroll said that the British authorities had turned down this suggestion. But he hoped they might reconsider it.

He went on to say that there had been too much compulsion in German education and that it was no use changing from totalitarian to democratic ideas if there were the same atmosphere of compulsion in the schools. "Education in the people's schools should be available to everyone. Teaching should not be too disciplinarian. Everyone should learn gladly, though it may take time even to learn to learn gladly and not to be brought up in an environment of iron and misery. Lessons should be made attractive. Quite a training will be required for German youth to get used to the idea of not being ordered about."

Like Adenauer and the professors at Bonn, he did not think that the influence of Nazi literature had been very great. He said that in all the public libraries there were cards at the end of the books recording how often each book had been taken out and read. It was astounding how few readers had interested themselves in Nazi books. The reason for this was that Nazi literature was too dull, humourless and dead to interest people.

Like Melchers, Kroll had ideas for starting a large publishing centre at Cologne: "We in Cologne must care greatly for books and produce many of them. We must have good newspapers, good books, good music, good literature. We must use our leisure well."

He had plans for German films and, lastly, a scheme for opening a French Institute in Cologne. Recently there had been found near Cologne a collection of 30,000 French books and 6,000 photographs, belonging to the German Institute in Paris. He did not know by what means the Germans had acquired these things. He supposed, though, that they were stolen. But he thought it might be reasonable to suggest to the French Government that this material should form a nucleus of a French Institute in Cologne.

When I left Kroll I felt considerably cheered. It seemed to me encouraging that there were men so full of ideas and plans for the future in the midst of this city which, as I drove across it, looked more than ever like a vast sandy waste of blowing dust, derelict walls and maimed monuments.

11. Nausea

A FEW DAYS LATER, I EXPERIENCED A SENSATION WHICH IS as difficult to describe as a strong taste or a disagreeable smell or a violent action, because, although it was a mental condition, its effects were so physical. It is worth endeavouring to describe however, because although I may have felt this rather more acutely than others, I believe that the condition is a mental one which is partly the result of the Occupation, and from which many people in the Occupying Armies suffer. Other people would probably explain the horror—the longing to get away at all costs—which affects the majority of the members of the Forces occupying Germany as a result of the ruined surroundings, the lack of entertainment and the generally depressing atmosphere. But I think that subtler and deeper than this is a sense of hopelessness which is bred of the relationship of Occupiers and Occupied.

The first symptoms of my illness were violent home-sickness accompanied by a sensation of panic that I would never get out of Germany. Home-sickness can be a constant and acute flow of unhappy sensations through one like an electric current: a current liable at any moment to emit sparks from violent shock. For example, I had one morning to see an officer to arrange for transport. On one side of his desk there was a bowl of sweet peas, on the other of red-hot pokers. This absurd floral combination gave me a peculiar shock of nausea because my wife's favourite flowers are sweet peas and we have a joke that mine are red-hot pokers.

Such sensations are acuter than most physical pain and, although they do not last, whilst they go on it is of little use telling oneself, what is most certainly true, that one will be better to-morrow, because they have the force of a vision and to say that one will recover from a vision is like consoling oneself for having perceived some reality by wishing to be blind or to ignore it.

For a day I was reduced to doing nothing but reading some French books I had brought with me, because everything in Bonn gave me a new pain. The flies, the monotonous explosions from the Rhine which shook the whole town, the band of subservient musicians who played "gemütlich" music in the dining-room while we ate meals each of which was more than a week's ration for a university professor, the preoccupied look on the faces of the inhabitants, the conversation of the mess—it was all a kind of dementia, a confused mixture of symptoms, disasters and evasions.

I lay on my bed reading André Gide's *Les Faux Monnayeurs*. I read this book because I had met Gide recently in Paris, because I had read it before and because occasionally I could recapture in it the very tone of voice of one of my friends in Paris. Why, though, when Olivier or Edouard said something which for an instant actually identified itself with the sound of the voice of some friend in Paris, did this console me like the sound of running water or like the music which penetrates into Florestan's cell in Beethoven's opera *Fidelio?*

The answer is that Germany is one vast monument or tomb of lost freedom and the voices which I heard were those of the free in spirit. My French friends would develop their ideas in the whorls of my ears even now while I was lying on my bed in a hotel bedroom of Bonn. Their plans, their thoughts, their relationships, their separate personalities, their future could grow in my mind where my affection could supply them with light and air in which to develop.

In Germany, however, it was impossible to create even through personal relationships this free atmosphere in which good could take root and develop. The Germans had deprived first themselves and then Europe of freedom and now they had made for themselves a prison and a ruin, and we were the gaolers.

The sense that the Occupying Forces are as helpless as the people who are occupied and that therefore the relationship between Occupiers and Occupied cannot be a good one because it cannot be based on the human impulse to help one's neighbour—that is what is depressing about the Occupation. The relationship can be one of charity, bribery, corruption, looting, Black Marketing, rape, all sorts of things: anything except free, mutual and creative.

At this point I should digress to answer the question: "Are you in favour of being kind or unkind to the Germans?" My answer is that the question is almost meaningless to me as I cannot ever remember having performed any act, kind or unkind, the sole motive of which was kindness or unkindness, though perhaps I have sometimes been influenced in action by the desire to be kind or unkind. Probably if the only considerations in our behaviour to Germans were kindness or unkindness, I would incline to unkindness for to remember what the Germans have done to other peoples, while one is in Germany, requires more imagination and more sense of proportion, than merely to be moved by the distress which one sees all round one.

The question of sentiment in our actions in Germany is scarcely ever relevant, and yet it continually arises. As a result of years of bitter hatred, many people are actually ashamed to perform some reasonable action because it might be thought kind and humane. Officers who tell you that their German employees are undernourished will explain at the same time that "that they hate Jerry as much as the next fellow does." Yet they need hardly apologize for wanting to feed workers who cannot work without food.

The administration of Germany should obviously be—and to a large extent is—based on policy and not on sentiment. It is a confusion of thought to explain—as is sometimes done—that our reason for feeding Germany inadequately is to punish Germans. Our considerations are really quite other than this. We have to supply other parts of Europe which have precedence over German claims, we have endless problems of distribution and transport, there are many shortages, etc. Why, then, invent an issue of sentiment which disturbs the minds of all who are working in Germany some of whom would like to be kinder, others less kind to Germans?

Sometimes confusion of thought actually influences our way of carrying out a harsh measure which is justified not for its harshness but because it is necessary. For example, we have to requisition houses while we are occupying the country. Requisitioning carried out on this scale and without compensation is a severe enough procedure. Just because it is so severe we treat it partly as a "punishment" and carry it out with a severity which in its turn we justify by saying that the Germans behaved still worse in countries which they occupied. Families had, when I was in Bonn, to leave their houses within four hours of a notice of requisitioning. They were allowed to take nothing with them except a few clothes and personal belongings which they could put into a suitcase, and a few kitchen utensils. If, when they had left, they urgently required any of their possessions they could then enter into a tedious process of applications through the German civilian and then the Military Government authorities to have some essential piece of furniture de-requisitioned.

Apart from principles of administration and policy and, indeed, often guiding them, there is a question of behaviour which arises in practice when the Occupiers meet the Germans. Here again it seems to me that a preconceived attitude towards all Germans is to a great extent dwarfed by two other overwhelming considerations. One is that Germany has involved herself in a general fate, a general retribution, and nothing can spare the individual German from this, whether or no he feels himself guilty. The other is that the individual German is an individual human being and although he has to suffer the general fate of Germany he is not exactly the same as all other Germans. He is either less responsible or else more responsible than others for what has happened, he has to evolve his own attitude towards events which have made him suffer, and to treat him in exactly the same way as one treats all other Germans is to do an injustice to his moral nature, an injustice which is not excused by the fact that many Germans (of whom he may not be one) have outraged the moral nature of other peoples.

Therefore, if I listened to people's grievances and self-justifications without producing the reply, with which, indeed, the stones of the whole of Europe seemed to cry out—"You have each one of you, to the same degree, brought all that has happened and all that may happen upon your own heads"—that was because I was not a stone, I am a human being and I try to treat other human beings as human beings even in a country which has brought down upon itself all the fury of the falling stones of a whole civilization.

Yet to think like this was to realize that there was almost nothing one could do. One could listen to people's complaints, one could explain that although one understood and sympathized, what was happening was the inevitable and that perhaps things would be better in five years. Once I was roused to explain to a professor and his wife that all their complaints were groundless, because the Germany of Hitler had called down upon itself, not an army of liberating angels, but simply the Occupying Forces, the Red Army, the G.I.s, the Tommies and the Poilus, with all the defects of the individual soldiers of whom these were composed. The Occupiers of Germany did not wish to be there, I insisted, it was the Germans who had invoked them. Nor did they want to stay; it was the Germans, in effect, who kept them. There was a silence in which I realized that I had definitely convinced my friends, then the professor's wife said: "What you say is quite true, and we should certainly never complain whatever happens." A moment later she added: "All the same, nowadays, sometimes there are moments when one feels extraordinarily depressed."

At the end of their gloomy, cavernous room which had once been a beautiful library there was a window looking out on to a tree which caught all the light on its leaves with an effect of brocaded richness, the richness of silks and cloth of gold which had not been destroyed. Sometimes when I was in this room with the professor and his wife, whose lives seemed to be ticking away in emptiness, like a clock in a cellar, I looked out at this tree which seemed to spring up with all the wealth of its normality, the resilience and power of recovery of life which is not condemned to suffer as a result of its own actions but which renews and forgets itself with each instant, and I longed to be outside.

It may be said that our discouragement had no significance, because after all in five or ten years conditions will be improved all over the world, including Germany. Yet I had experienced the same kind of discouragement as now in Germany in 1931, in Austria in 1935 and in Spain in 1937. On each of these occasions I could have reminded myself that it was not necessary to be depressed because the conditions I saw were only temporary and in so far as they were bad they were remediable. There was no inevitability about the war. The very fact that it was so obvious in its approach provided dozens of occasions for averting it. If politics were a medicine chest of social remedies applied to the ills of society there would be nothing to disturb us in the evils of our time, for we possess all the means for remedying them. But the disease is not in our surroundings, it is in ourselves, the doctors, and thus we do not use the remedies which exist in our surroundings. In our time the necessary measures to deal with an avertable disaster are never taken because the self-sacrifice, disinterestedness, co-operation and realism necessary to meet approaching dangers can never be achieved until nations are actually engulfed by them. Politics is, rather, a perpetual application of half remedies to disasters which have been foreseen and which might well have been avoided. Meanwhile new disasters are visible on the horizon and everyone realizes what should be done to avoid them but the necessary unity of purpose to avoid them can only be achieved when it is too late.

Thus everyone speaks to-day of a "German Problem." Yet there is no ability to solve this problem as a whole, because the famous "German Problem" is not the problem of a defeated Germany to-day, but of a warring Germany of yesterday and perhaps again to-morrow. It is obvious that if a "German Problem" existed to-day it would perforce be solved with the same resolution as it has been solved during two wars this century, and the symbol of such resolution would be a unified policy of the Allies towards Germany. As it is, all the talk about the "German Problem" is an excuse and an evasion, a blind for the fact that there is for the time being no "German Problem" and that, therefore, no attempt is being made to solve it. Germany, instead of being a place where the "German Problem" is being solved has become a scene where the disunity of the Allies is projected and one more demonstration of the fact that modern states are incapable, during what is called peace, of sacrificing national sovereignty in order to avert foreseen disasters.

Thus the enervating peculiarity of this modern political age is the extent to which we are constantly confronted with disasters which might have been avoided and offered opportunities and solutions which are refused. The war which Churchill profoundly suggested to Roosevelt should be called the "Unnecessary War" could have been avoided, just as the next war can be avoided. But since war is implicit in the peacetime commercial and national system to-day, Churchill might have gone one step farther and labelled our modern world the "Unnecessary World."

The purpose of this digression is to justify my sense of nausea on certain days in Bonn. My depression was caused by the sense not just of a temporary condition around me in Germany which could be remedied by programmes of Reconstruction, but by the realization of a real potentiality in my environment, as vivid as the potentialities of Nazism in 1931. This was the potentiality of the ruin of Germany to become the ruins of the whole of Europe: of the people of Brussels and Paris, London and New York, to become herds wandering in their thousands across a continent, reduced to eating scraps and roots and grass. It was the sense as I walked along the streets of Bonn with a wind blowing putrescent dust of ruins as stinging as pepper into my nostrils, that the whole of our civilization was protected by such eggshell walls which could be blown down in a day. It was the sense of two futures within modern humanity, like the two worlds within Faust's breast, one a future of confidence between people in a world of such happiness as can reasonably be organized within the conditions of human existence, the other a world given over to destruction and hatred. Both these potentialities were real: but the constructive one required resolution, unity, will, acceptance of guilt and a conscious choice to determine our future, the destructive one was to be got by going on as we have done now ever since 1918.

12. Lieutenant Arran

AT THE TRANSIT MESS AT BONN THERE WAS AN AMERICAN officer who had the exceptional privilege of being able to entertain. His name was Lieutenant Arran. He lived in the Mess but he worked in the suburbs of the town where he was provided with American rations of such a handsome scale that he was able to invite five or six visitors to every meal. The meals were served out of doors in a pleasant verandah which jutted into a garden of flowering trees and shrubs. The garden had not been tended for some time and was agreeably wild.

Arran was a Southerner, with the pleasant Southern drawl. He had dark eyes and hair brushed back which rather overemphasized the smooth roundness of the lower part of his face. He was quiet in manner, interested in everyone, generous, humorous and prudent. He was a shining example, in fact, of the great American virtues which are as rare among Americans as are the best national qualities among the members of any nation, with the result that the more we see of English, French or Americans, especially when they are away from their homes, the less we see in them their national virtues. The worst ambassadors of most nations are its citizens abroad. Since we have seen a great deal of the American abroad lately, we have lost sight of the American virtues. Above all, Arran impressed one by his unobtrusive desire to understand everyone's point of view, qualified by a determination not to be taken in.

The first time I went to lunch with Arran, he explained to me that he did not speak to Professor S——, the proprietor of the house, which was an institution of the University with laboratories attached to it, because S—— was a Nazi. "I don't think he ought to be kept in his job and I think we're far too nice to these people. When I arrived here I had only one interview with Professor S——. I said to him: 'I want you to behave as though I were a German officer billeted on you, a civilian.' He understod perfectly what I meant, I must say. Since then he's just stood aside respectfully when I come along the corridors and he never says a word to me." Lieutenant Arran grinned reflectively as he told me this, rubbing the side of his chin with his hand.

I said: "I know that S—— was a Nazi, but the official reason for not dismissing him is that he is an expert on malaria and we are unable to dispense with his services."

"That may be so, but all the same I don't see why we should be so damned polite to a man with his record. I believe in being very reserved indeed as far as indispensable Nazi members are concerned."

"I quite agree with you. Once we admit that some Nazis can be given privileges because they are useful to us, our whole position of maintaining that there is something evil in Nazism is endangered, because it means that we only treat Nazis as they should be treated when we can afford to do so. We conduct a vindictive campaign against the very prominent Nazis and also against the insignificant ones, but we leave all the middling ones who are probably the most important and certainly among the most responsible."

I pointed out that the other professors in Bonn objected strongly to S——, partly because, apart from their professed hatred of Nazism, they were seriously afraid that if the English Occupation were given up, men like S—— would be in a position in the University to victimize those professors who had collaborated with us, and who had already been victimized throughout the Hitler regime for their democratic views.

Arran took the view that the Nazis were still a menace. He was sure that they were firmly established within the German sections of Civil Government. He concluded this not only from observations of the Germans but from what he knew of "our people and your people," as he called them. He was not in favour of revenge and brutal methods (though he had, as I must say I had also, a sympathetic attention for the feelings of people who had really suffered abominably from the Germans), but he was in favour of coolness and strict justice, as far as we ourselves were concerned. Like many soldiers who had fought against the Germans, he was left cold by the sudden switch-over from treating the Germans as enemies to treating them as "just like anyone else." I felt that he disapproved of my fraternizing, even with the professors of the University, though later on his attitude rather altered.

Arran had been left in Bonn, for some reasons which I do not know, to run a printing firm which was issuing school books. He treated his German workers with fairness and detachment. They liked this. And when, a few months later, he left Bonn, some of them actually wept.

It occurred to him that while German children were being provided with school books, nothing was being done for the re-education of the young people in the Displaced Persons'

Camps. He tried therefore (with what success I don't know) to have school books printed for Poles and Russians which could be used in these camps.

There seemed to be nothing extraordinary about Arran. In fact he had qualities which suggested honest ordinariness. Yet it is exactly such unblinkered open-minded attentiveness and interest in one's surroundings which appear to be most rare. His ordinariness was his sane gift of seeing things round him in a true and objective way. Sometimes, when he was with boring or pretentious or silly people, he had a way of looking at them with his wide smiling yet a little withdrawn gaze, which had the effect of exposing the tangled places of their minds.

With Arran there was always the warm sense of homecoming which one feels in the presence of people who really care for truth. Problems dissolved themselves into humanity. If people spoke about Russia or about Displaced Persons, Russia ceased to be a sinister projection of our fears and her fears, and became the Russians, certain people with certain characteristics living in certain conditions which could be understood and which it was most important to understand. Displaced Persons, instead of being gangs of destitute criminals unjustifiably wandering about marauding and robbing, more disliked by the authorities because more of a nuisance to them than the Germans, became what indeed they were: victims driven out first of their own countries and then of any civilized existence by the Germans.

Arran had, in fact, the critical spirit. One has only to move in Europe to-day to realize how rare this is. Many people simply judge every issue by their own interests, many others by what they think to be standards of national pride. Then there are those who have some standard of sentiment which they consider sacred: that is to say, they wish always to act or think in a manner which presents them in a most favourable light to themselves. There are people who pride themselves that they are incapable of an unkind thought, for example, which means that they are lying both about themselves and about other people to themselves. In Germany there are plenty of people who wish to appear unkind, because they think that they have a righteous reason for the first time in their lives for being as nasty as they really are, and of course they do not wish to lose this opportunity of unfettering their inner natures. The unkind people lose their tempers if you point out that a family living in the cellars of Dortmund is starving, and then they accuse you of not sympathizing with the people of Warsaw. Even more trying are the people whose self-esteem seems to depend on their always depicting themselves to themselves and to others as kindhearted. For example, I remarked to a well-known young pacifist in London that the Germans were, in my opinion, for the most part, rather neurotic and difficult to get on with to-day. He immediately protested "*I* never find it difficult to get on with anybody; you see *I* treat everyone as an individual and *I* love everyone. And the result is that everyone loves *me*." I could hardly resist the temptation to say: "Well, I don't." Of course, his own ideas of himself being the only principle of feeling or behaviour for him, it was not necessary for him, in asserting all this, to know anything about the behaviour of the Germans. It may at least be said for the people who hate humanity that they have some reason for doing so whereas the professed lovers of humanity usually love no one except themselves.

Then there are all those people whose minds are hopelessly divided or confused, and those quite honest people (most of the ordinary soldiers) who are either too humble or else too corrupted by opportunity, to trust or to act on their inner judgment. Moreover, in Germany there was the political issue of "good Germans" and "bad Germans" which most officers were unable to grasp. Many officers expressed the view to me that on the whole they sympathized with the Nazi because, after all, he was a fellow who stood up for his country, whereas the refugees were rats who had let their country down. That good men could thus identify themselves with the evil of the S.S. would seem incredible unless one made allowances for the complete ignorance amongst most people even to-day of what the Nazis stood for. A colonel who had come to Bonn from the 21st Army Group asked me attentively what I thought we should do in Germany. I suggested that, amongst other things, we should do more to encourage the anti-Nazi elements. He said: "But surely that would be very difficult. Do you mean to say that we should take sides in this country?"

The very fact that most of the officers who made remarks of this kind were well-intentioned and efficient people, carrying out difficult jobs well and cheerfully, makes it the more striking that they had no grasp of the longer and larger picture of which they were a part. The most industrious and well-meaning people tumbled into all the traps: the trap of hating the D.P.s because they were "a bloody nuisance," the trap of respecting the Nazis because they were patriotic and efficient, the trap in short of judging every issue by its immediate effects on their own work and not by the relation to past and surrounding events. Perhaps if I had been embroiled in actually having to deal with the nuisance of D.P.s and Nazis and non-Nazis, I also would have taken up the same point of view. In fact, later on, when I had to open German libraries, I was to discover how difficult it was in practice to insist on maintaining the distinction between Nazis and non-Nazis.

Thus it was a great relief to be often with Lieutenant

Lieutenant Arran

Arran, who did not share the blindnesses and prejudices, the general conspiracy of allowing the compromise of action to become a perversion of one's point of view, of nearly everyone.

It was even a relief to go in his company to a Variety Show staged by The Theatrical Company of the Guards' Division, called *The Eyes Have It*. This revue was an expensively produced third-rate imitation of a third-rate West End revue. It was distinguished in writing, acting and staging by a complete lack of originality and of the faintest semblance of vitality. Everyone approved of it in the way that he approved of everything which did not fall below a certain standard but no one could have gone away from it stimulated by any touch of imagination, any touch of beauty, any touch of understanding, any touch of genuine amusement. I was very irritated by all the time and expense which were wasted on actors who went round in the uniform of Guards' officers without their being capable of providing the men who were living in such strange and difficult circumstances with any real refreshment or pleasure. All the Guards' Division company could produce was a hackneyed imitation of the men's own idea of what they were supposed to like. Probably that was not the fault of any of the people immediately responsible. But it seems to show a lack of energy and imagination somewhere which is characteristic of our institutions.

One evening Lieutenant Arran and I stayed up rather late at the Transit Mess and got rather drunk in the company of some Russian officers. The Russian officers who had seen *The Eyes Have It*, concerning which Arran was being studiously reserved, announced, after they had drunk a good deal, that they would give a show for us. We thought they were joking, but, at once decided, they were quite serious. They said they invited us at the same evening in two weeks' time to a variety show which they themselves would organize at the largest Displaced Persons' Camp in the neighbourhood.

13. Rudi Bach

IN THE COURSE OF THE NEXT WEEK I WENT TO THE HOSPITAL to see Rudi Bach, the boy on whose behalf I had written to the Town Major asking him if he could obtain some penicillin. As soon as I arrived at the hospital I found that I was quite famous with all the staff as the Englishman who had enabled the hospital to try its first cure with penicillin. At least four doctors gathered round me in the entrance hall of the hospital. They thanked me profusely for having obtained penicillin. They took me up to Rudi Bach's room and while the boy lay in bed staring at us with large leaden blue eyes through his dead white face, with his motionless hands laid outside the bedclothes on the turned-back sheet, they lectured me on his illness, illustrating what they were saying with X-ray photographs, each of which was thrown down on the boy's bed when they had finished with it. Once, the boy (whom I watched more than I did the photographs) took up a negative of his enlarged heart and looked at it closely with a kind of soft attention. The doctors told me (all the time in front of him) that he was suffering from a septicæmia of the heart and that the chances of recovery were nil. They did not believe that penicillin would make any difference, but it was true that his condition had improved astonishingly during the past twenty-four hours since he had started taking it.

They knew very little of penicillin and little enough even of sulpha drugs. They questioned me eagerly about these things explaining that they were dependent for information on the wireless, as they had no medical journals. They asked me if I could tell them about the effects of insulin used as injections in cases of lunacy. Unfortunately, I knew nothing of these things.

It was quite impossible to say anything to Rudi Bach, because in the small ward for two patients there were the four doctors, his mother on guard beside the bed and the other patient, whom everyone ignored, an old man with a parchment face and with knees drawn up under the bedclothes almost to his chin. The mother was a voluminous and voluble woman who kept on apologizing to me for the fact that Rudi would not show gratitude sufficiently to his benefactor.

The next morning I called at the hospital again. His mother was at Rudi's bedside once more and she at once started interpreting him to me. He was very much better. She said she would like to bring me some fruit, an offer which I accepted. I gave Rudi a book with comic drawings by Wilhelm Busch which I had managed to obtain. He said it was "prima" and he started looking at the pictures in it at once, without looking at all at me. His mother snatched the book away from him, and said it was rude of him to read it *now*, meaning when I was in the room. I said that I had written my address in the end of the book and that he must write to me when he was well enough to do so. I told him that when I was sixteen I had been very ill and that my legs had been completely paralyzed but that I had got better and since then I had never been ill again. As I said this I remembered that it was exactly this kind of thing which people said to me when I was so ill and how it had irritated me.

14. Displaced Persons' Concert

THE DISPLACED PERSONS' CAMP WAS ABOUT FIVE MILES OUTside Bonn. It was a large grey modern village of straggling stone or concrete houses built on a slope alongside a road of stone and mud, and rather ineffectively cut off from the rest of the countryside by a number of sentry posts and barbed-wire fences.

Nothing could be more depressing than these grey slotted houses like dominoes, in roads alongside a slope which was not a hill but a broad upwards unrolling of the whole landscape which looked like an irregular football field of grass hacked to mud at the end of a dull wet season.

The houses like dominoes lying on their sides were for officers. A few of these Russian officers stood about on the side of the road in their stiff coarse jackets braided with wide strips of gold on their shoulder straps, and in their tough breeches, the texture of whip-cord. Away from the road, on the mud slope, there were peasants. Hundreds of them, timeless peasants, exactly the same as in Tolstoi or in Turgenev, only transplanted here, as though into a foreign zoo; women with their cheekbones which made their cheeks protrude like apples, ripe apples for the young ones, wizened ones for the old ones; old men with shrewd sunk eyes in shrivelled faces and with beards like curling fur on animals, beards which had never been touched by comb or scissors. There was a bedazed atmosphere of incomprehension of their whole situation, and at the same time of dulled monotonous carrying on with their miserable prison tasks.

What filled me with awe was the sense that these people were human beings of a species having nothing to do with their surroundings. They had transported their environment with them and set it up in reduced, miserable, tattered form, a wretched caravanserai in the midst of this bleak alien environment. The slave labourers, in their vast herds in Germany, look like human animals who have been put in a foreign zoo out of which they broke at the time of the Occupation, to be caged up again, though less completely, by the Liberating Forces. There are some wild ones who break out every night and prey on the surrounding countryside, instigated partly by misery, partly by a primitive spirit of revenge.

We walked slowly up the hill, feeling ourselves suddenly to be very important, royalty or visiting deities almost, compared with these people, the slaves who were now worse off than slaves, having been freed to become a mass whom no one wanted. Indeed, we were gods or kings or anything we wanted to be in relation to them, for, in comparison with them, we were infinitely free, with our meals at the Mess, our cars that brought us here, aeroplanes which would take us back to England. There was less social gulf between the King of England and myself than between these people and myself, because the fact that one is, comparatively speaking, a free agent gives one social equality with other people who are free agents. Inequality is lack of freedom, imprisonment, slavery, extreme poverty.

At the top of the slope, there was a large long wooden hut which we were shown into. The inside of this was like the interior of a vast dank barn, with the soil as floor and a damp earthy smell coming up from it, and above that smell the stifling gaseous smell of unwashed people. About a third of the floor space was covered with benches. Behind these benches there was just an empty space. The benches were crowded with people sitting and the space behind was full of standing people, waiting and talking. It was like a tent on Bank Holiday, full of disconsolate, derelict people. A few half-naked chidren, all of them with short-cropped hair which showed that their little heads were covered with scabs, crawled about on the ground. Some members of our party started playing with a little boy aged about three and taking him onto our knees. He reminded me a little of my son, aged six months, who is also partly Russian. But when we saw beyond his enchanting smile to his verminous condition, we quickly pushed him away, with a feeling as though we had trodden in some filth.

We were shown to places barricaded in our honour from the rest of the audience. A few people on the benches nearest to us showed a slight interest in us. But to most of the audience, our presence was simply a sign that the show should begin. As soon as we were seated, they began to clap and to shout for the curtain to go up. There was quite a long delay, of course, before it did so, and during this interval I began to sense the electric interest of the audience in the performance. It was like an audience of children at a pantomime waiting to be mesmerized by a magician, transformed by transformation scenes.

The curtain went up, revealing a stage almost as bare as the auditorium—one could have wept for the bareness of it— furnished only with a dozen or so chairs of the kind they have in institutions, a threadbare upright piano and some dirty curtains as backcloth. A man who had the leathern stolidity of a hippopotamus in a cartoon by Walt Disney came forward and started declaiming in a loud voice. Behind me, a very young Guards' officer with blond hair, ice-blue eyes and no chin started jeering, clapping his hands and shouting ironically: "Hailsky, Trotsky," etc. The fact that the speaker spoke Russian seemed to him in itself utterly ridiculous. After the man had stopped declaiming twenty stalwart girls marched onto the stage. They stood in front of the chairs (which were later on the seats of a band) with the fixed staring attention of people waiting to be photographed in 1860. In unison they produced a song which seemed to be played with perfect discipline on a large out-of-tune metal instrument.

Of course, the ash-blond Guards' officer sneered more and more. But afterwards there were things which silenced even him. There were two excellent male dancers who did the old-style Russian peasant dances of squatting down to the ground and kicking their feet out. There was a strangely dignified woman in a worn-out ball dress who danced a solitary sweeping waltz. There was a shockingly bad violinist. Some very vigorous songs, written by members of the camp, were sung: these were ballads describing ironically the progress of Hitler in Europe. They brought the house down. A Russian interpreter by my side translated these songs for me.

Then there was a little farce about the manager of a theatrical company who has to interview certain actors and singers for the purpose of their playing certain rôles. His assistant is a clown. This clown, half-man and half-woman, fantastically dressed in brightly coloured rags, equipped with a broom, a handbag and a large scarlet nose, was slightly terrifying and amazingly animated. The whole of this farce was acted with a vigour and spontaneity which communicated itself instantly. One had the illusion of understanding what the actors said.

The contrast between this show and *The Eyes Have It* produced by the Guards' Division was so striking that it is impossible to ignore. The Guards' Division, with whole-time actors, released from almost all their other duties and with actresses imported specially from Brussels, with elaborate scenery, with power to requisition theatres, and with special vans for transport, was incapable of producing a show which expressed one original idea, or created one fresh gesture or piece of scene painting, one story not a prefabricated chestnut. These unfortunate D.P.s, with no books, no scenery, bad instruments and very little talent, had managed, within a fortnight, to stage a performance which, despite glaring deficiencies, was full of originality and imagination, and which, above all, carried the day by the sheer force of its vitality. If, without any other evidence, one had to judge the two respective civilizations, the Guards and the D.P.s on these two characteristic productions of their respective cultures, one would have said the British were a civilization where a culture of conventional respectability was lapsing into banal obscenities, that the D.P.s were a primitive civilization with an amazing force of imagination and crude improvisation amounting to genius.

15. Dinner Party

THE EVENING AFTER THE D.P. CONCERT, I WENT TO ONE OF Lieutenant Arran's dinner parties. I took with me a young man called Aulach who was the strangest inhabitant of the Transit Mess.

From a long time before I spoke to him, I had noticed Aulach and wondered who he was. Dressed always in civilian clothes, he never spoke to the officers and never dined in our Mess, choosing to sit alone at a table in the Privates' Mess. He was tall and thin with sculptural bones which seemed to carve their shapes through his flesh. He was extremely pale. His face had a white transparency which gave it refinement, especially as the features went very well with such a marble pallor.

He had a proud, remote, yet not hostile or unfriendly expression. He used often to look at me and for a long time I half-wished to talk to him, but my sense that he was a complex and difficult person inhibited me, as I felt that if I became involved in any way in his affairs I would have no easy escape from him since he lived at the Transit Mess.

So it was not until a few days before leaving for England that I spoke to him. He at once told me an involved story about his situation. He had lived all his life in Germany, but his parents were anti-Fascist refugees, both of whom had acquired foreign nationality. He was now almost twenty-one and in the position of being able to choose his nationality. He had chosen not to be a German. He was now waiting at the Transit Mess while long negotiations were going on to enable him to join his father abroad. This is enough of his story to explain how it was that he, though born and living all his life in Germany, was at the British Officers' Transit Mess.

Aulach said he hated all the Germans. He did not wish to remain in Germany and he felt himself to be a foreigner there. His mother was an aristocrat of the family of von H——, which Aulach for some reason said "was the most famous anti-Nazi family" in Germany. His father, of Jewish origin, was an artist now living in Paris.

Aulach was at present occupied in interpreting for the British officers controlling forestry. He claimed therefore that he knew what the ordinary Germans were really saying, since he worked with them and they accepted him as a German. He said that the Nazis were getting quite cheeky and were satisfied with the behaviour of the British authorities towards them which was favourable beyond their expectations. In fact they had very little with which to be dissatisfied, since most of them, as middle men, were still in powerful controlling positions. At present they looked forward with confidence to a war between the Western Powers and Russia, which they regarded as inevitable, when the democracies would look to them for aid.

He said that amongst themselves the Germans scarcely discussed any political topic except the next war. The elaborate political parties with democratic liberties attached to them adumbrated by the Allies were regarded as a Debating Society for backward children, and these backward children, the Germans, were living in conditions which made them interest themselves either in much closer or else in much remoter topics.

During the war Aulach had been employed (he said) in the German branch of a Swiss firm which made batteries for U boats. He said that this firm, by faking results of experiments, managed to delay the invention of batteries which would enable U boats to remain under water for periods of up to three months on end. He said that the inspectors whom the Nazis sent round to factories were idiots and nothing was easier than to impose on them.

I was interested to know what Arran would think of this curious character.

The dinner party consisted of Arran, two A.T.S. girls, Captain Jim Raven (an officer with the serious, kind expression of a progressive farmer), Aulach and myself. One of the girls, called Elizabeth Aitchen, looked specially smart in her neat uniform, with her hair done in such a way that it looked pressed and moulded over her head as if it were part of her uniform. There was a metallic gleam about her coiffure which strengthened this impression. This girl was well made up with large, cold, shining eyes impooled in lashes like the feelers of an insect and with a determined, painted mouth through which she uttered decisive and stupid remarks in an extremely refined accent.

The dinner party did not go well, largely through my fault, I think. Indignation about *The Eyes Have It* had put me in an opinionated mood in which I rather "forgot myself." I said almost as soon as I arrived that although the despised D.P.s had no resources, their show was a hundred times more alive than the Guards' Division performance. Miss Aitchen said nothing but looked furious. I asked rhetorically why it was that the organizers of entertainment for British soldiers were, nearly all of them, incapable of producing an original idea or even a pretence of anything lively and interesting. How was it, I asked, that actors in uniform could get privileged positions as members of a Divisional Theatrical Company, whereas almost no use was made of the writers who might produce some extremely interesting and original literature around a life of the army, Fascism, war?

As I said all this, I had an awful sensation of coming out in my true colours. The presence of Aulach in some way contributed to this and made me go farther than I might have done, if he had not been there. Arran was diplomatic in the way that I found almost touching in him. He said in his slow voice with the Southern lilt that *The Eyes Have It* didn't strike him as in any way original but that it was a performance which reflected much credit on all concerned, and he added that there were certainly occasions in his life in which he had been more bored than during the interesting evening when he saw the Guards' Division entertainment.

Jim Raven said in his mild kind countryman's voice, looking at me inquiringly: "But if you went home directly after the D.P. show, you didn't see half what we saw, Stephen."

"What did you see?"

"You remember the young Guards' officer with very fair hair, pale blue eyes and no chin who sat behind us?"

"Yes."

"Well, he and two Russian officers showed us the prison

cells after the performance, in order to show us round all the sights of the place, I suppose."

"What were they like?"

"It's rather difficult to say, as they were almost in darkness. But we were taken into a shed which was rather like a long stable with a corridor, out of which doors led into cells like stalls. It was all very rough and primitive. First, as we came in, we were shown a cell in which there were about ten women packed closely together, lying in a heap alongside each other on the ground. The Guards' officer explained to us that these were people waiting to be sent back to Russia where some of them would be shot, some sent for long term imprisonment to Siberia. What surprised me most, was that he explained that in this cell some of the women were condemned to death, but others were shut up with them in the same cells who were only charged with quite trivial offences such as going out of the camp for a couple of hours without a pass."

"What was there in the other cells?"

"In another cell there was a Russian collaborator, a man with a beard who looked like an old peasant. He was going to be hanged. The Guards' officer, who seemed to think all this very amusing, said that sometimes people from the camp came in and made this collaborator entertain them by walking about on all fours and barking like a dog."

"But who is responsible for all this? The Russians or the Guards?"

"The Guards are only responsible for protecting the camp, the Russians are responsible for the conditions which exist there. All the same, I must say that I was rather surprised," Jim Raven said in his impressive, ruminating way, "Very surprised in fact."

Elizabeth Aitchen said in her refined indignant voice:

"They are all like animals, the Russians and the D.P.s. They aren't human beings at all. We oughtn't to treat them as though they were human like ourselves."

Jim Raven answered: "The Russians would probably explain that they have no space for better accommodation for their prisoners. They can't house and feed their people who aren't prisoners even. And in any case, I believe that the very fact of being a prisoner and having worked for the Germans at all makes the D.P.s highly suspect by the Russians, which is, after all, understandable, though it is all rather grim. I suppose, too, that they express their feelings about collaborators in a rather primitive way."

"Well, I can understand that they don't feel inclined to treat their collaborators gently," said Arran.

"In my opinion you can't judge the Russians by our standards at all. They simply aren't civilized," said Elizabeth Aitchen.

Arran took this up quietly. "That's quite right. You certainly can't judge them by our standards. You have to understand them by their own standards, and if you do that you're beginning to get somewhere. That is why I myself, speaking personally, make such an effort to get on with them, I think it's worth the attempt."

"How would you behave towards the Russians then, Arran?" asked Jim Raven.

"For a beginning I'd send them as much as possible of everything we've got. Food, clothes, equipment of every sort; then lots of refrigerators, gadgets, watches: all the things they want. Then I'd admire them tremendously. Before I explained to them how civilized we were and how admirable was our democracy, I'd explain how much we needed the experience of their civilization and to understand their point of view. And at the same time I'd be very clear about certain things: very clear and very firm."

After this the conversation wandered rather. However, instead of letting it get on to film stars, I inconsiderately brought it back to Germany. Arran's point of view interested me so much that I wanted to go on questioning him.

"It seems to me," Arran said, "That the next war is being prepared right here, right now. And it won't necessarily be the kind of war which everyone talks about, of the Germans against the rest. It may well be something quite different."

"On the other hand, we can stop it here," I said.

"Oh, but you'll never stop wars," said Elizabeth Aitchen warmly. "It's natural for men to fight. They wouldn't be men if they didn't fight."

Her friend, the other A.T.S. girl, supported her: "I don't think that a race of men who never fought would be much use anyway," she said, looking at me viciously.

"Unfortunately, if there is another war, it will certainly destroy civilization," I said. "Therefore we must do our best to stop it happening."

"So. You have come to Germany because you believe that it is possible to prevent wars by taking some kinds of action, improving conditions, removing the causes of war, planning a new world, founding a society of nations," said Aulach. "You are quite wrong, you'll never succeed."

"My idea whether I'm right or wrong isn't based on my certainty of success," I said. "I simply don't want all this to spread. I don't want the whole world to be transformed into the ruins of Germany, and I think it's right for me to do my best to prevent this happening."

"You are wasting your time," Aulach said. "Nothing will

stop it happening. The world is doomed. You can't obstruct the development of history."

"We are history. Human consciousness is history. Anyone who puts an idea into the heads of his contemporaries to persuade them to take an effective social action has influenced the course of history."

"That's where you're completely wrong. History has nothing to do with the conscious will of people living at a given time, for the simple reason that there is no such conscious will which can affect the whole course of events. History is the development of the unconscious mind and life of humanity which is a stream flowing from the past and leading into the future. The wills of men and women living at a particular time are not a decisive bend in the stream of life, they are just straws afloat and carried along by the stream which consists of the unconscious life of the sum of the whole past and future humanity. At the moment the human stream is falling over a precipice and we are being carried over the precipice by it. There is nothing that we can do."

"If there is nothing that we can do, there is still nothing to be said against our doing our best," I said. "I am not interested in the idea of a history outside our wills. If there were such a kind of history I would be against it. I do not object to being historically unfashionable. I am interested in doing my best according to my lights."

"That is quite wrong also," said Aulach. "In a time such as the present the only way in which to be strong and real, to exist in the fullest sense, is to realize within oneself the dynamism of the forces which are bearing the whole of our civilization to destruction. Your point of view is completely superficial because it is only concerned with your conscious will.

That is to say, it is a frustration of the deepest forces within you which are forces of chaos and destruction."

Arran managed to steer the conversation away from these gloomy depths. He had a way of not arguing with his guests but of just cheerfully accepting their views as a contribution to the general interests of life. I was somewhat bemused by Aulach and so I concentrated on my food, which was the best to be obtained in Bonn. When I listened next to the conversation I heard Jim Raven say to Arran:

"Do you consider that President Truman is as irreplaceable as Roosevelt was considered to be?"

To which Arran replied in his slow, slightly sententious voice: "Well, if there is one great virtue which Mr. Truman has, it is undoubtedly to be the most replaceable man in America."

Arran and I then started discussing books which one would like to write (he knew vaguely that I wrote but had never seen anything I had written). He said: "There's a very good book to be written about our life out here. I mean, not a big book about all the great causes, but a close observant book about all the things that happen."

Shortly after dinner I left, as it was my last evening in Bonn. I had said good-bye to one of the professors but had forgotten to return some books to him. I was anxious to give them to him before he retired to bed. At the same time, I felt that I should not go, leaving Aulach whom I had brought with me: so I suggested to Aulach that he should walk with me to this professor's house.

It was a very stormy evening. Before we had gone a hundred yards heavy rain began to fall, so we took refuge in a tunnel under a bridge of the railway for half an hour. At the end of this time though it no longer rained so hard, the storm was not over and flashes of lightning lit up the town which, a moment later, was plunged into darkness. These dramatic white flashes made the ruined walls look flat like grey cardboard. The wind rattled through the hollow buildings with a noise of flapping rags and of rattling tins. The roofless half of Bonn absorbed with a purring sound the rain which flooded rooms and soaked through putrescent rubble as through a sponge. A damp, heavy, oversweet sickening smell began to rise from all the ancient rubbish heaps along the roadside.

This dramatic setting was an admirable background to Aulach who talked about himself without stopping, and louder than the thunder. He explained to me that he was half-Jewish, half-pure Nordic, so that he incarnated in himself the ideological struggles of the Third Reich. His Nordic personality hated his Jewish personality, his Jewish personality was continually trying to sabotage his Nordic. His Nordic side was creative, bold, bad, generous, ruthless; his Jewish side was analytic and self-destructive. His Jewish side prevented his Nordic side from being as ruthless as it would have liked to have been. Evidently there was also a super-ego in his make-up, a kind of third Aulach who was a detached observer standing above both these contestants which heartily took the side of the Nordic Aulach against the Jewish Aulach. What he hated most about his Jewish self was its habit of questioning the activities of his noble, fearless, mystical, creative, intelligent, Nordic self.

Aulach said that the Jews were not only uncreative but also incapable of arriving at any conclusions even as a result of their analytic researches. I suggested that Einstein had perhaps arrived at some conclusions. He replied that Einstein was the most destructive spirit of the age who had attempted to build up a system of Jewish ideology to undermine all the crystallizations of the creative Nordic spirit, by making any fixed point of truth untenable.

Meanwhile it had started pouring with rain again. I was afraid all the time of being late for the professor so we pushed on through this storm. When we arrived at the professor's it was dark and no one replied at first when I opened the door. At last he appeared, wearing a dressing-gown. I thought that at least he would be amused at or appreciate my being soaked through but he looked disgruntled, particularly as Aulach was with me, and he did not ask us in. He took the books and said "Good night." I realized that he was a man who liked every moment of life to be lived with art, and it was painful to him that our last meeting before my departure from Germany should be in these circumstances.

On the way back through the storm, Aulach went on talking. He told me that at Heidelberg he had belonged to a group of students who discussed philosophy all night long. He had been chosen to make a speech at some annual function and he had given an address which had offended the Nazis. When he was a boy he had injured his back and had to wear a steel support but he had nevertheless won a race. Aulach went on and on like this. He was not stupid, he was not boring though rather tiring. Why did I feel that he appealed for sympathy and that yet I could never be able to help him although I did care and sympathize? I can only answer that question by turning away from Germany and considering my relationships with people who are not Germans and not living in Germany.

French Interlude

MAY, AUGUST AND OCTOBER 1945

1.

THE PEOPLES OF THE WORLD TO-DAY EXIST IN A STATE OF anticipation of their being precipitated into a new pattern of unity or a new chaos. The whole of civilization is enclosed in one idea: the idea of the potentiality which may recreate everything or destroy everything. This colours the mind of everyone who thinks. The visions of the fate in which we live and of the future before us are stronger at times than the reality of our actual surroundings.

We are familiar with the idea of the end of the world. It is quite possible for us to imagine the towns in which we live being pulverized to the condition of the towns in Eastern Europe and of Germany. Indeed, sometimes it is difficult to imagine this *not* happening. The idea of destruction exercises a fascination over many minds to-day. Many sensitive people begin to abandon ideas of reconstruction for the acceptance of the idea of a destructive fate. They scarcely wish to belong to a social order and a material environment whose laws and even whose physical structure only maintain themselves by a postponement of the day when they will be destroyed. For it becomes evident that the inner life of humanity has attained the power to transform completely and totally the outer environment, so that the chaos or the order of that inner life must inevitably be reflected in man's future environment. Thus we find in literature a growing insistence on *being* rather than on making.

There is an Either-Or choice before men to-day which in the past was only real to religious thinkers whose minds saw life as an eternity where there was a separation of humanity into the good and the evil, heaven or hell, on the day of Judgment. But to-day we are confronted with the choice between making a heaven or a hell of the world in which we live, and the whole of civilization will be bound by whichever fate we choose. Moreover, it seems that we have to make the choice: we have to decide one way or the other; we cannot abdicate from the position of having to choose.

We are confronted with this choice between creation and destruction immediately after a period in our history when it had seemed that morals were simply an affair of private conduct and that no necessity of making a moral choice confronted the whole of society. The characteristic of modern industrial society was surely the transference of responsibility for government first away from kings and aristocracies, then away from governments, classes and even nations, to a mechanical interaction of forces directed by certain interests of class and wealth. No individual was wholly responsible for events in a world where policy was the direction of many interrelated actions, and where any one act produced such widespread repercussions throughout the entire world that it became absorbed at once into results which developed beyond and in different directions from the initial action. Even revolutionaries aimed at transferring power from one set of organized interests to another, rather than at simply overthrowing kings and governments. In this world where no one was responsible for society, it seemed that a synthesis of competing self-interested motives would result in the survival of the fittest and the general benefit of mankind. This most modern industrial society looked to the pattern of evolution of man from the ape before the dawn of history for the pattern of its own development.

In this society, although many people shared a general sense of guilt for the injuries it inflicted, and though there were many acts of atonement and reform, no one felt personally responsible for the events around him. No individual could take upon himself completely the sins of the industrial revolution. Saint Francises of the *rentier* class who gave their all to the workers were only proving in another way the inefficacy of individual action, the unreality of individual responsibility. A sense of enlightened social irresponsibility became a sign of the intelligent adaptability of artists. It became stupid to think— for example—that literature could exert an influence to change society: books can perhaps influence the hearts of men, but they cannot influence a social automaton. All the arts could do was to save a few individuals from becoming as mechanically minded as other people in the age in which they lived by opening their eyes to other kinds of reality.

But to-day the situation is completely altered. It becomes evident that the social automatism of conflict between interests, nations, classes, individuals, which it had been hoped would add up to a general progress and improvement of the whole social machine, has developed means of destroying itself in internecine conflict, unless a majority of the peoples of the world assumes complete and conscious responsibility for the future pattern of the world. A new pattern of world society designed for the end of securing peace must come into being with the consent of all the nations, and peace must be more important than national interests. The world must be modelled

French Interlude

according to the necessities of the future peace and world-unity and not according to the supposed necessities of existing interests. Since we have become accustomed to accepting the idea that all arrangements are adjustments of existing interests, which can be calculated in terms of power and wealth, the step before us seems almost impossibly difficult to take. We have got to set the whole *human* interest in front of the existing power-and-wealth-interests, at a time when we have almost abandoned thinking of politics in terms of humanity.

We realize to-day that what goes on in men's minds may have a terrifying effect on their environment. The nihilistic nightmares of Fascism have proved that, and the weapons which destroyed Fascism have proved it to a degree which makes even Fascism seem a childish dream. We approach a phase when the whole consciousness of contemporary humanity affects and is responsible for the present environment and the future development of humanity (if it is to survive) to a degree never imagined before in the days when one could have confidence in the intractability of nature and of *things*. Man's power over nature is reaching a stage when his wishes and fantasies can quickly be transformed into potentialities for good and evil sufficient to transcend completely or destroy completely all existing arrangements. The secret weapons of Hitler and the atomic bomb of the Allies were the first warning of this phase against which there is no protection.

Defence has been the secret watchword of humanity until 1946. Man has always been defended against the extreme consequences of the chaos of his inner nature by his inability to impose his own shape on reality or else by his own ability to invent counter-measures which neutralized the effects of his own violence. In the past the religious view of life has been based on the assumption that the struggle between good and evil would continue throughout man's lifetime, but without a decisive victory being won by either side. The decisive victory was left to be arranged in the next life. But we are now entering the era when man is defenceless against himself, when nature is defenceless against man and when the dream of the shape of an after-life suddenly becomes real in this life here and now.

No wonder that to many people it seems that our civilization has entered a final phase of King Lear on the Heath. When it seems possible for man to write *Finis* on his world, it seems, from what we know of him, and from what we see taking place in the world around us, unlikely that anything will prevent his doing so. Moreover, there is a strangeness and newness about the apocalyptic time in which we live, time of great destructive and great creative resources, which we cannot accustom ourselves to. It blinds us and fatigues us as though by exposure to a too great light which shows ourselves to ourselves and *the others* to ourselves with all too much truth and reality. The citizens of every city in the world know that their city is held together from moment to moment, stone on stone, either by mere postponement of a day of reckoning or else by an act of faith.

Fortunate people, hearing the cries of the fallen and of the wandering herds of the less fortunate in Europe, ask themselves by what strange chance they preserve their good fortune, and how long they will continue to do so. They are brought always back to the realization that the inner forces of existence are suddenly revealed as the supreme forces on which the external future of civilization will depend, just at a moment when men were consoling themselves for the decadence of the inner life by remembering the systematic development of science. All those old prophecies of burning cities, trancendent powers and of a final choice between good and evil seem to be fulfilled

French Interlude   92

in us: those prophecies which point with equal clarity to two worlds: a world destroyed by fire and a world created by the human spirit.

2.

PEOPLE ARE THUS IN THIS SITUATION OF REQUIRING UNITY and a general sense of responsibility at a time when Western civilization has been split up into peoples living under very different and hardly interrelated conditions after five years of war. Although there is one danger threatening all and one solution possible to all, yet all find themselves in different situations. Some—defeated Germany for example, and ruined Poland —are further gone down the road than others. Others—America, in particular—are isolated by their victory and prosperity in a position where it is very difficult for them to appreciate the position of the ruined countries. Yet perhaps the ruined countries are nearer to the reality of our time, which is that it is necessary to think out a new world from the beginning—from their zero.

After five years of the breakdown of communications through war there has never been a time when countries were so isolated within their own separate experience, and yet never a time when they shared so completely the same realities.

One might compare the countries of the world to-day to clocks. Each country registers a different time, but outside their time there is one time for the whole world, registered on one clock, with a time-bomb attached to it. Unless the countries of the world can synchronise their time and their sense of reality, that time-bomb is likely to explode. The one hope for the world is that many people in all countries should realize that they are equidistant in time from a disaster which will affect all if it is allowed to happen. For it is only the recognition by all of them—the prosperous and the poor, the victorious and the defeated, the socialist and the capitalist—that they are at the same distance in time from an event which may destroy civilization, which can save them all.

The countries of the world are isolated in their separate experience. Yet, the pressure of awareness is so great that the world to-day has a kind of transparency. We look through our own experiences to those of other countries. They might be us and we might be them. What has happened to us might happen to them. Through the streets of London and Paris we see the streets of Hamburg and Warsaw. Yet, it is easier in Paris to imagine the whole city being destroyed, than in Berlin to imagine Berlin being rebuilt.

The very fact that some cities in Europe still subsist has become a kind of miracle which adds tacitly to the emotion of the traveller in them. The Frenchman travelling in England feels not only that this country was for long years the fortress of a Europe not utterly defeated so long as we remained but that the physical survival of nine-tenths of London is a victory over chaos. The immunity of Paris from destruction has the strength to the English visitor of far more than material presence.

And all the time, behind London, Paris, Prague, Athens, are those shadows, those ghosts, the destroyed towns of Germany which are also the part of the soul of Europe which has collapsed visibly into chaos and disintegration. Their ruin is not just their ruin, it is also pestilence, the epidemic of despair spreading over and already deep-rooted within Europe, the

French Interlude 94

black foreshadowing of the gulf which already exists in us—
the gulf which we can still refuse.

3.

MY FIRST VISIT TO FRANCE SINCE THE WAR WAS IN MAY
1945. I was invited under the auspices of the British Council
to give a lecture (or Conférence) in a series of reunions between
French and British intellectuals. The director responsible for
my reception was Austen Gill, then head of the British Council
in Paris. With great understanding, he encouraged me to treat
my visit as little as possible as a public duty, and as much as
possible as a means of making personal contacts.

Thus I spent my first two days seeing no one, re-discovering
Paris. The question whether Paris is the most beautiful city in
the world is somewhat idle. But it is the city of modern times
whose beauties most have an air of spontaneity and inspiration
without their being an accidental agglomeration of beautiful
things like most other beautiful cities of Europe (though it certainly contains many accidental beauties, particularly in the
Latin Quarter). Paris springs at one and away from one with
all its converging and radiating avenues, like an impulse of the
mind. It provides the eye with pleasure and with a sense of
triumph because one looks at it with a sensation of seeing how
it has been made; one sees it everywhere as the expression of
an idea, of problems stated and beautifully solved. It is a perpetual stimulus to its inhabitants and its visitors because it
suggests for ever the possibility of shaping and making in an
idiom and with materials not too remote from the possibilities
of our own day. It does not belong to an age whose possibilities

are not ours, like the Akropolis or Venice. It is a city which one can for ever discuss and which inspires to creation. Its inhabitants are not overpowered by it, nor does it become their implicit uncommented background. They watch Paris for ever with a discussing eye, catching it like a woman unawares in moments of surprising beauty and stimulated by it to thoughts and creation of their own.

Speaking in bad French, I gave my lecture (at a hall whose name I forget). It was on *The Crisis of Symbols in Poetry*. In the poetry before the Industrial Revolution (I said) poets would readily derive from the Court and the Church symbols such as the Crucifix and the royal Crown, in which the conceptions of power and glory in this world and the next were united and concentrated. Such symbols when they are used to-day derive their strength from the fact that they once had an emphasis which they lack to-day in our age of constitutional monarchy and belief in Science. The modern world of power uses a specialized technical language. It is impossible to find in it public symbols which unify concepts in the manner of the old symbols. Yet the old symbols are weakened by their association with institutions which have become weak in contemporary life. I quoted a poem by Thomas Hardy called *The Oxen* which has for subject that Hardy can no longer feel the Manger and the Oxen at Christmas as unifying symbols where the power of another world brings its radiance of comfort to this one. In this modern world of specialization in which there are no unifying symbols (unless the atomic bombs) the poets seek either boldly to use a modern environment of factory and slum symbolically, or else they try to invent pure unattached symbols devoid of association with either the past or the present, objects of contemplation around which meanings accumulate like the visions in the glass of a crystal gazer.

French Interlude

This lecture, in which I discussed modern poetry around this central idea, was a strange experience. For one thing, the chairman introduced me in the most extravagant and embarrassing terms. Whilst he was talking I was analysing my own feelings at being introduced in this way. I found that actually I disassociated myself completely from what he was saying. He was not talking about me, nor yet, though, did I feel exactly as if I were a member of the audience listening while he was talking about someone else. He was talking, as it were, about a rôle which I could not seriously be expected to fill but for which the audience accepted me as a token. Whilst he spoke, I felt like an actor waiting in the wings.

The social position of a writer, especially of a poet, is curious. Officially and commercially (as I discovered during the war) to be a writer is to be a vacuum which the social structure abhors. Three examples will illustrate this. In my passport, under the heading *Description,* I had put my profession as *Poet and Journalist.* This is actually copied into my passport, but a rubber stamp has cancelled it and written above are the words *Government Official.* My second example is that when, during the early part of the war, I applied for a job in the Ministry of Information, I was unable to be recommended for it, because the interviewing officer discovered that as I had never passed any examinations, I had no qualifications for filing quotations from newspapers, which was what the job demanded. Later when I was interviewed to become part of an AMGOT mission for putting the British point of view across to Germany the chief interviewing officer of a committee representing the War Office, the Board of Education, the Ministry of Information and one or two other Ministries, said, on hearing that I only wrote books and did no "serious journalism": "You seem to us to be the kind of person who never sticks to anything."

Thus, for most of my War Service I was a fireman. This is all quite understandable, but it would have made the chairman's speech about the tremendous importance of modern poets in our civilization sound rather strange, had I not decided in my own mind that this speech had no connection with me at all.

The lecture was made still stranger by the fact that there were in the audience several people whom I knew but whom I had not seen for many years. There was Sylvia Beach, James Joyce's publisher and owner of the Bookshop Shakespeare and Co. in the Rue de l'Odéon, together with her friend Adrienne Monnier, who also runs a famous bookshop, and with two young men whom I did not know but whom I recognized from descriptions of them—Maurice Saillet and Michel Cournot. There was Madame Ghisa Drouin, formerly Ghisa Soloweitschik, whom I had known in the 1930's when I was living in Berlin at the same time as Christopher Isherwood. Isherwood and I used to go every Sunday to lunch with her and her parents. The family is described in a story of his called *The Landauers*. At the end of every Sunday meal, they used to stuff our pockets with fruit, because they thought that we were almost starving. For Isherwood always complained about his extreme poverty, though in this story he makes out that he resented Fräulein Landauer (Ghisa in real life) giving him things which he did not want. At the end of *The Landauers* Isherwood describes how Fräulein Landauer was transformed by meeting her fiancé, M. Drouin, now in my audience seated beside her. Shortly before the war, I had seen the Drouins in Paris. It was a very pleasant evening, in the course of which we had spoken of the approaching war. M. Drouin said: "It's easy for you English to talk about resisting Nazism. But it is France who will suffer in this war, as she did in the last. It is France who will be devastated. England won't be touched."

In the audience I could see also my translator, Marcelle Sibon who, years before the war, had heroically tried, without success, to publish my work in France. In a way, this occasion must be a triumph for her, I thought. I had last heard from her in the summer of 1940, during the invasion of France, when she had taken part in the flight from the German armies. She had written to say that after what she had seen she would never have any sympathy with the Germans again. There was Patrice de la Tour du Pin, the poet, to whom I had been introduced immediately before the meeting, who, as I knew, had been in a prison camp during much of the war. There was Henri Hell, critic, and assistant of Max Pol Fouchet, editor of the magazine *Fontaine* whose numbers, published in Algiers, had been an inspiration to the writers all over the world who cared for freedom, during the war. Max Pol Fouchet had visited London during 1943, when I had seen much of him, and when he had organized for *Fontaine* the publication of a number devoted to English literature. There was Professor Bonnerot, a professor of English at the Sorbonne, who had done a great deal to acquaint French readers with English poetry before the war, and who during the war had carried on a clandestine correspondence with Charles Morgan.

Thus everyone there had his history which invisibly had reached and affected me during the long years of darkness and war. There was a feeling of reconciliation about the meeting, which had nothing to do with the chairman's speech, nothing to do with my lecture, though both of us were trying to do what was required of us. So much had happened, there was so much to explain. England had not gone unscathed. Instead of sacrificing France and then making peace with Germany, she had borne the brunt of the war for long months. Thus for many Frenchmen England had become the vindication of an idea which, in previous wars, it seemed that the towns and soil of France and Belgium alone in Europe had vindicated. This being the basis of our understanding, there were a dozen personal bonds of an interest between us which had grown without our necessarily having met, during the war. How often, for example, after having read his poems, and having heard that he was a prisoner, I had thought of Patrice de la Tour du Pin, during the war, and of Sylvia Beach, and of the editors of *Fontaine*. In a diary of 1943, I had copied out some remarks about poetry from *Fontaine* which I now found were by Henri Hell who became one of my best friends in France. I had known his thoughts for four years already, and I was united to friends in France and to friends in Europe by what amounted to bonds of prayer. And now these friends expected England to strike such another note as she had done in 1940, and to lead Europe out of a second abyss.

4.

THE FIRST PEOPLE WHOSE HOSPITALITY I ENJOYED WERE THE Drouins, probably also the last with whom I had dined six years before in Paris.

They gave me all too excellent a meal—five courses of things collected together with difficulty. It was a pleasant evening; M. Drouin sat on my right, at the head of the table, Ghisa on my left, and their little boy aged eleven, with his bright puckish schoolboy face, sat opposite me. But there were shadows. It was more than that everybody looked so decidedly older and more worn. The Drouins told me that one of their children had had to go away to friends in the country as a result of strain and nervousness resulting from these years. Ghisa and I talked about the old days in Berlin, and about Isherwood.

Then, of course, inevitably, we talked about the Germans in Paris. All through the Occupation, Ghisa had had to wear the Cross of David, as she was Jewish. She was only allowed to sit on certain benches in the public parks. In the Metro she had to stand in the part of the train reserved for Jews and Negroes.

This part of the Metro, she said, was always crowded. For there were always people who went there, in order by doing so to express their sympathy with the Jews.

The Parisians played practical jokes on the Nazis. One day, for example, many dogs of Paris wore the Star of David.

Ghisa was only allowed to go into shops (wearing the Star of David) at certain hours in the morning. In order to keep her family, she had to trespass outside these hours. This meant going into shops without her Star of David. If she had been caught doing this she would have been deported. Then we started talking about the deportations. And at this point the little boy Georges interrupted and told us how a comrade of his at school had been deported, together with his grandmother, and never heard of again. Then there came a look on his face which made us change the conversation.

We spoke of other things. I told them a little of life in England. I told them about my own work, about Auden and Isherwood having gone to America, and so on. But I had the sense of something irreparable having happened. Everything had been altered. What really gave the sense of this alteration between us was the realization that life is harnessed to inexorable laws of destruction and to the perversity of human nature. The Nazis had taught a whole generation of people in the world that they were no longer young and that they could not foster the hopes that young people have.

Sometimes, when people in the occupied countries speak of the Germans, one has the sensation of a sob of fury and despair. One realizes for a moment the extent to which the Nazis were entirely destructive and that their programme for destruction included the destruction of the possibility of human forgiveness for the Germans themselves. These wicked children had set out to damn themselves entirely, to exceed the seventy times seven of offences for which it is possible to forgive human nature. Thus often one has the impression when talking about Germans with non-Germans in Europe that one is not talking about human beings. One is talking about the monstrous, the unutterable, the thing which hundreds of people all over Europe never wish to hear mentioned again.

"How did they behave?" I asked Marcelle Sibon on another occasion. "Did you stumble on them lying sprawling drunk all over the Place de la Concorde, like the Americans?" "Oh no, they were not in the least like the Americans. They were perfectly correct, perfectly correct." She laughed, with sudden hardness: "Only, every morning one read on large posters in the Metro, beautifully printed in type like a page from a Lutheran Bible, the names of about thirty Frenchmen whom they had shot at dawn." "Did they appear to be happy?" "Perhaps just at first," someone said. "In 1940, when they appeared to be carrying everything-before them, including our hearts. But then what was extraordinary, for years and years, was the impression they produced of utter misery. At times it was difficult not to be sorry for them," the French voice said with contempt.

There was also the corruption they had left behind them.

French Interlude

"For four years," Professor Bonnerot remarked sadly, "we have made a virtue of cheating the Germans. The result is, I am afraid, that now that they have gone, we continue to cheat ourselves. We envy you English because you have the sense of civic responsibility which seems to be lacking entirely in our country." Not only cheating but also suspicion and inequality of wealth were among the tares sown by the Germans in France. People suspected their neighbours of having collaborated. No one knew where the large sums of money which many people had to spend came from. Before the Germans left France they flooded the country with paper money. Thus, amid conditions of poverty and distress, there were many people with large sums of money unaccounted for. To check this, the government during May called in all the banknotes over a certain value at a certain date, to be changed for new currency. At the same time everyone had to declare and account for his money. A few days before the calling in of the money many people purchased books, furniture and other expensive objects with banknotes of high value.

France is a country where everyone is being tried in his own conscience and in the eyes of his neighbours for the part he played in the war. People who collaborated or who are suspected of collaboration undergo a certain amount of social persecution though many of them still enjoy the advantages of having collaborated. An English visitor is constantly being warned that he should not meet So-and-So and So-and-So. He may find after accepting an invitation to someone's house that he has been lending a little of the prestige of England to someone who has formerly borrowed heavily from the prestige of Germany. Paris is full of social dangers of this kind. The higher you go in society the more you find that people are compromised.

5.

THERE WAS THE SENSE OF MEETING AGAINST THE BACKground of five years of war, bitterness and corruption. In all personal relationships, I found that the feeling of reconciliation, amounting for me to revelation of the qualities of France, predominated. Everyone I met clarified, explained, gave their best and did their most to be understood. With the French writers I had less than ever before the sense of there being barriers between us of nationality, of language, and above all of this indifference to the need of making any real effort to understand each other which usually divides people when they have achieved a certain measure of maturity and success.

During my visit to France I met several very different kinds of people but they all had the same need for meeting.

Sometimes I remember this sense of meeting simply as the expression of a face. For example, the eager, open and friendly expression of Patrice de la Tour du Pin, who told me of his imprisonment in Germany, of his home in the country where he lived alone with his wife and where he wrote his poems, of their baby, and so on—often tales mixed with incidents of difficulty and discouragement, but always with a look of such friendliness that he achieved always the gaiety of a creative attitude—that is to say, of an attitude which treats everything in life at the same time seriously and as a story-teller's joke. Sometimes it was an act of generosity, as when I discovered by chance that our host at this luncheon had sold a sofa to pay for the lunch. Sometimes it was the serious effort of someone to explain himself: of Francis Ponge, for example, the writer of prose poems of a curious stillness and objectivity like still lifes in words, explaining to me that rhythm and music do not matter (a view which I do not share); what mattered was the crystallization of meanings around one object on which the poem was concentrated, "and whether one is Ponge or Spender, even if one writes thirty versions of a poem, not one of those versions must be written carelessly, because a careless phrase, or an insight wrongly observed, runs the risk of introducing a false note into the final poem." Or it might be Loys Masson, the communist Catholic poet, originating from Mauritius, and a member of the Resistance during the war, explaining to me how he had become a communist through having seen for many years the oppression of the workers first among the natives and then in France. Or it might be Vercors, discussing the German problem with great attentiveness, convinced that there must be Germans with similar views to our own, and that eventually co-operation between Germany and the rest of Europe must be achieved.

In Loys Masson I met a type of French communist who was new to me. He seemed extremely reasonable, undogmatic and open-minded. His communism was that of a man who, although he hated violence and dictatorship, had been driven to the conclusion that without a violent transference of power from the hands of the present owners to the workers, it was impossible for the conditions in which the workers, and, even more so, the coloured people lived, to be more than superficially changed. He was aware of the truth of many of the criticisms made of Russia, but he thought that French communism should not be judged by Russia. The Russian revolution, he said, was essentially Russian in all its features and results.

The French, Masson said, had a great tradition of individual liberty and he did not think that a communist government in France would suppress this tradition. I replied that I was sure that he spoke in good faith and I believed it likely that many communists in France thought like him. Many Frenchmen, even those who were not members of the Communist Party, felt —as I had noticed—that the Communists were the only party with a realistic grasp of France's position and who were capable of the strong action necessary to France to-day. Had not even Professor Bonnerot said to me that he thought the only means of stopping the Black Market would be to appoint a Communist Minister of Food?

Yet, I went on, the Communist Parties in all countries were essentially directed from the top by leaders. Communism could not be judged by the goodwill and good intentions of individual Party members but by the behaviour and directives of leaders. Did the Communist leaders in France show a really different spirit from those in other countries? If not, was not Masson himself in the position of a dupe in supporting them? Masson said this might be so, but in what other way than communism were the freedom of colonial peoples and the public ownership of the instruments of production to be achieved? Of course, I could not answer this satisfactorily. We were both face to face with the unpleasant reality that fundamental social change means loss of the liberty of the individual, for a long transitional period at least. And what guarantee have you, I asked, that liberties lost will ever be restored? When have transitional tyrants ever voluntarily declared that the period of their transitional dictatorship is over and that they are now willing to abdicate? There has never been a world in which the temptations of power were greater than the world of to-day, because the modern tyrant has in his hands instruments of tyranny far more powerful than ever before in history, and, if in the modern state the individual once loses his liberty, it seems impossible for him to regain it unless through intervention from another state outside.

French Interlude

André Frénaud, the poet, who had been imprisoned for some years in Germany, who was present at this argument, took my side. We all agreed as to ends, we disagreed only as to means. Although I could not agree with Masson, I realized that he was a person who had been brought far more closely in touch with the practical workings of capitalism and imperialism than I had. This did not make him more right than myself but it made me respect his point of view in a way more than I did my own, because his was hammered out of harder experience. He saw the urgency and necessity of change and his eyes had the expression of a man who multiplies every second lost to social justice by the suffering of millions of men and women, which he realizes with his whole being.

Yet a comparison of France with England to-day and with the rest of Europe to-day, makes one realize that an atmosphere of freedom requires a certain amount of respite from the exigencies of hard reality such as dominate nearly all the existence of Eastern Europe. France, whose entire economy and politics have been systematically and deliberately undermined by the Germans, is an *invisible ruin*—to use the word "invisible" in the same sense as in a phrase such as "invisible exports."

At the back of everyone's mind there is this sense of an unacknowledged zero which France has reached, from which the community has to be completely reconstructed, just as Germany has to be reconstructed from zero. But although the sense of this pervades the atmosphere, meanwhile the walls stand, the cafés are crowded (although there is no coffee) and there is always the Black Market. All this might seem inexcusable escapism (and does seem so to many Frenchmen) if it were not for the fact that there is also—dependent on the game of going to Black Market Restaurants—the world of ideas, of art, of personal relationships. France still remains the centre of such interests—she is the market place of the human spirit, the central world exchange of civilized values—and this spiritual life fulfilled on a fashionable, amusing, intimate, pleasurable and worldly plane in Paris, is dependent on material things, even on a certain amount of corruption.

What strikes the visitor to France is the extent to which people deplore the situation without doing much, if anything, to improve it. You are talking to a friend in a café. A friend of his who has just arrived from Algiers pauses a moment to say good evening and that he is inexpressibly disgusted with all he sees in Paris, nods, and then passes on to say the same thing at the next table. You constantly find yourself being congratulated on the admirable "civic spirit" of the English, but how few people try to emulate this spirit. Perhaps it is impossible to do so, and this is a point worth considering. One day I met at a tea party a professor from the Sorbonne whose suit was twice too large for him, and he explained with a wry smile that he had been living for two months without recourse to the Black Market. The point is that it is possible in England to be adequately nourished and clothed without recourse to the Black Market. And this has always been so since the beginning of the war. It has been possible to distribute our resources evenly over the greater part of the population. Therefore with us the Black Market has been a safety valve rather than an organized system of wastage. But if at any time, we had not been able to obtain our rations and distribute our resources, there would almost certainly have been the same Black Market problem here as on the continent. Thus the parallel which the French draw between themselves and ourselves is not entirely just to themselves. And there is a certain facility about the way in which they condemn themselves which is almost as disquieting as the evils they deplore.

French Interlude

The material situation in France does not seem by any means insoluble. It is a comparatively simple one of economy, discipline, work, and the general recognition and acceptance of what is necessary.

Yet beyond this apparently simple question of arrangements, the whole French way of life is in the balance and an old conflict between the spirit of Protestantism and the richer Catholic tradition lurks. The question for the French is not just: "Do we have to tighten our belts and work harder for a few years?" Beyond this, there is: "Do we have to abandon the fusion of sensuous with spiritual experience, the synthesis of which has been the great French contribution to the art and culture of the modern world, for a grim, realistic, ascetic revival of the spirit alone based on a recognition of France's defeat and of the fact that France is as ruined as the rest of Europe?" "Do we have to turn away from the conception of the individual, sensuous, social, bound up with other individuals through an acceptance of his whole physical and spiritual nature, to the conception of the isolated individual among the ruins, the saint, the puritan, the prophet, the extremist social revolutionary, the enemy of pleasure, and the accepter of bare exigence for our future?"

Far beyond the frontiers of France there are the countries reduced to a condition where the way of life which makes French cultural values possible has been completely destroyed. And the question is whether it has not been destroyed in France also. Whilst many Frenchmen postpone the recognition of this, there is also perceptible in France the growth of a puritan Protestant movement (whether it is amongst Protestants, Catholics or communists), which accepts it. There are signs of such an acceptance of France's position in the renewed demands that

French Interlude

literature should be "engaged" with social problems, in the essays of Jean Paul Sartre:

> The writer is situated in his time: each word has its reverberations, each silence too. I hold Flaubert and Goncourt responsible for the repressions which followed the Commune, because they wrote not a single line to prevent them. It may be said that it was none of their business: but was the case of Calas the business of Voltaire? the sentence on Dreyfus the business of Zola? the administration of the Congo the business of Gide? Each one of these writers, in some particular circumstance of his life, weighed up his responsibility as a writer. The Occupation has taught us ours.

Here, although Voltaire is quoted, the most striking feature is the denunciation of the writers preoccupied with problems of pure literature, Flaubert and Goncourt. It goes without saying that the communist writers, from their different angle, have the same point of view. So for that matter do the severe and responsible Catholics, such as the critic Albert Béguin.

France is a country where you meet many people who would die to-morrow on the barricades for an ideal in which they believed. Indeed one of the powerful forces in French life is the uneasy death-wish of some of the younger men who feel that they did not play a sufficiently glorious rôle in the Resistance and who would now welcome some opportunity to prove their courage to themselves. And yet these same people lack the force of what they call "civic virtue."

Although they are themselves ashamed to admit this, perhaps the struggle which is going on in their conscience is not so ignoble as they think. They are divided because while they feel themselves still to be the old France they are conscious also of their fate being bound up with that of the rest of Europe. As a Polish writer said to me: "We writers of the East of Europe feel a certain bitterness when we meet you of the West in Paris and London. We feel that something has happened during the past five years which we in the East cannot escape from, because it has become our whole environment. We are surrounded with it on every side. It is our starting point and it is what prevents us from developing. Then we come to the West and we see that you are pretending that you are still living in 1939. Everywhere we see an inflation of unreal ideas!"

6.

BUT WHICH IS REAL? DOUBTLESS IN FRANCE TO-DAY THERE IS a pervading sense of unreality. It is unreal to avoid acting in a way that recognizes the facts of France's weak position in a world which is still one of Power Politics. It is unreal to treat concrete problems as though they were unreal nightmares, or unpleasant family gossip universally talked about but never recognized in action as the shape of France as she is.

Yet although France may be weak in the world of Power Politics, she remains the most valuable asset of our culture and civilization. It is the consciousness of this which makes it so difficult for the French to accept their situation. But the failure to accept it results in a certain debasing of the French virtues, a poisoning of them at the root, of which everyone is conscious. To illustrate this at its crudest, the whole of French cultural and spiritual life subsists on the Black Market, from the fine paper on which beautiful books are printed to the food eaten at restaurants where people exchange ideas. Perhaps it is necessary to accept this situation. But inevitable results of it are fury and cynicism.

Thus at this moment when almost everyone in France tells

you that France is eternally disgraced and whilst the politicians talk of French prestige, one is poignantly aware of French virtues. They are the virtues of self-knowledge and maturity, and because the knowledge of the self is, in part, of the self as a social being involved in the general social despair and corruption, cynicism is often accompanied by the greatest generosity and selflessness. The French never strike one as being good because they have remained immature and have not learned better than to be good. Their honesty, generosity and kindness are not the results of failure to appreciate the bad qualities in their neighbours.

In Paris, I met several of the young writers, some of whom I got to know rather better than the more famous and more busy ones. One of these was a critic, K——. As with other people in France, I found that once I had K——'s confidence he was self-revealing in a way that I scarcely imagined people could be. That is to say, without being self-absorbed, he knew everything about himself, he accepted his own personality profoundly, with calm and clarity, and without seeking to impose himself on other people. Often when we were together with other people, I noticed how little he tried to make any impression on them. If people were indifferent to him or disliked him, he accepted this also as a fact about them and about himself. Having a strong sense of vocation as a critic, he was very sure of his own judgments, particularly about literature and music. He claimed always to be completely objective and he asserted that his aim in life was "lucidity." This amused me at first, because I thought that it was impossible to be either objective or lucid. But I gradually found that objectivity and lucidity meant that he applied the very exactly-defined limits of his appreciation with great clearness to every experience. This meant that in fact he was always quite sure of his reasons for liking or disliking everything and he could feel with confidence that he was not swayed in his judgment by personal reasons. His love of beautiful things was real, his appreciation generous. Ultimately perhaps his idea of himself as completely lucid and objective was a myth, but since it was applied within strict boundaries within which it was possible to be perfectly clear, it worked. Moreover he had a passion for clearness and honesty in his conduct and in his relations with other people which gave him the serenity of a person of good faith, which had a calming influence on everyone round him. "Like me or dislike me, approve of me or disapprove of me," his manner seemed to say. "You are quite free to do either. I make no plea for your sympathy or your approbation. All I want is that you should make up your mind and that we should be perfectly clear in our own attitude towards each other. I quite understand that in every human relationship and in everyone's attitude towards everyone else, there are infinite possibilities of hatred and love. And I am quite prepared to accept this freedom of choice. I do not demand that people should approve of me. All I ask is to know where I am."

When people take a clear, detached, yet affectionate attitude towards the world around them, one is confirmed in their company in one's own appreciation, because their judgment has the value of free uninhibited choice. To go about Paris with him, to go to the Louvre, to walk along the banks of the river, to hear him read aloud the poems he loved, was to enjoy everything twice as much as I would have done alone. It was an essential part of his personality that he loved pleasure also, in fact *"le plaisir"* came high up in his hierarchy of values as definitely defined as a chart in his character. It was not just that, liking goodness and beauty, he could also do with a good deal of pleasure; it was that pleasure was inseparably fused for him with goodness and beauty. And talking one day of the spiritual and the physical aspects of love, he said: "I'm sure of one thing, and that is that I know my own nature. And I know that, for me, the physical and the spiritual aspects are inextricably bound up together. If the physical is sacrificed to the spiritual or the spiritual to the physical, there is a maladjustment of my relationship with someone I love."

It is easy for a person with a confused nature to sacrifice (or at any rate to enter into undertakings to sacrifice) one side of his nature to the other. But someone whose conception of his personality is whole knows that in giving up one aspect of his personality he is affecting the other. Pleasure in a well-balanced nature is not just pleasure, it is also sanity and goodness. The philosophy of life of a great many Frenchmen has been based on a recognition of this, and a result of this recognition has been that French art has been at once the subtlest and most solid contribution to the values of our civilization. At the moment, when the defeat of Germany has been followed by a wide-spread diffusion of German idealist and romantic ideas all over Europe, this is an unpopular view; but, so far as I can see, it remains true.

After meeting many French men and women, I began to think that French novelists are very lucky in having the French to write about, because there is a definition about the motives of the French which is lacking in those of other people. The Frenchman's complete self-knowledge makes other nations accuse the French of cynicism, just as the fact that we, the English, suppress in ourselves consciousness of our bad motives causes foreigners to say that we are hypocritical, with the result that many foreigners interpret policy in the Empire and other parts of the world by the simple process of seeking out and naming the motive which the British never mention.

The French novel contains a very close interpretation of

the character of the French individual in whom several lines of motivation develop, as it were, horizontally, though, at times, they converge. Thus one can read French novels not (as with the classic English novels) to look at outstanding and colourful characters, or (as with the novels of central Europe) to see people exposed by revealing situations, but to recapture the way of thinking, the very tone of voice of one's French friends. In Germany, I often used to read French novels, when I was feeling depressed, for this very purpose. The French novel is "psychological" not in the sense of making profound analyses of neurotic conditions, but in that of delineating very precisely the lines of motive and behaviour which go through the life of individuals who have a great self-knowledge and a great acceptance of the conditions of human existence.

7.

IN MAY, AFTER STAYING IN PARIS, I WENT FOR A FEW DAYS to Toulouse and Montpelier. There was some mistake of reservation on the train, so that I had no place. I found then that every seat in the train had a ticket attached to the rack above it, to say that it was reserved. The French reserve places for every long journey now, though to do so may necessitate standing in a queue at the railway station for as much as six hours. I lay all night in the corridor, which was very crowded also. At about six in the morning I was woken from my half slumber by a lady being sick over me.

I felt so exaggeratedly happy that in a sense it was a pleasure to share these discomforts with the other passengers in the corridor. I thought of "lucidity" and "objectivity" and decided that I should not attach importance to insignificant things. I had been reading a novel called *L'Etranger* by Camus, whose scene is amongst the Arabs, and I imagined myself to be an Arab going on a journey of many days in an overcrowded cattle truck full of other Arabs. This Arab, whom I thought myself to be, had spread his blanket or cloak on the floor, and was seated on it, with his legs crossed, and he had made his mind as blank as a desert. In this way, I spent the journey with a pleasurable sense of transferring myself into an Arab.

When I arrived at Toulouse, a loudspeaker on the platform announced that I would be met at the station entrance.

The station was very animated. Some of the other passengers on the train were deported prisoners returning to France from Germany and Austria, where they had been working for the Germans. Most of them were dressed in shabby blue-grey and each carried some kind of kit-bag. The fact that they were given an official welcome with a band at the station did not seem to add materially to their gaiety. In fact, they seemed not to notice these arrangements at all. One saw from the look on their faces that they were part of something far too vast. They belonged to that great sea of lost anonymous people flooding over Europe who have been so torn away from their past that few of them can find it again. They may transform Europe into their own uniform greyness and dullness, but they cannot be absorbed back into our civilization by a brass band, a tip and perhaps a suit of clothes. They are the lost.

I was welcomed by M. Ponsoll, with black hair and black, iron-rimmed spectacles, a solicitor (I think) and a most solicitous host who took me to my room in the station hotel. It was like a room in a station hotel in a French film. Water was not laid on and it had an air of coherent drabness which was not without charm. The large long bay windows looked out over a

French Interlude

view of railway lines, a road running by the side of the railway, an iron bridge over the railway. Noises of wheels, steam and whistles rose from this scene with the vivacious plaintiveness of the cries of gulls. The air was sooty and grubby but its smoky edge was gilded by a sun quite different from that I had seen in Paris—the sun of serious intent in the south where the day's business is to be light.

I asked if I might rest until noon. So I got into the bed which was large and such an appropriate setting for two lovers, one of whom has deserted from the Foreign Legion whilst the other is a waitress, and I slept till I was called by M. Ponsoll at noon. Then I was motored to a villa on the outskirts of the town where I was given a stupendous banquet by the members of the Anglo-French Association.

In the afternoon I wandered around Toulouse with M. Ponsoll. Toulouse is a town where green and rose mingle in a picture whose pigments are ancient red brick and gardens run wild after years of war. The one house built of stone in Toulouse is a sightseer's curiosity. There are great red-brick houses with courtyards and gardens behind them, towers and halls, all built of this brick which has acquired, with the years, the texture of soft red cliffs flaking off into petals.

At six o'clock there was a party given at the Maison des Intellectuels, a Left Wing organization which originated, I believe, at the time of the Front Populaire and the Spanish Republic. This party was like all parties, there were many interesting people who formed a crowd and one was dazed by the feeling that it was impossible for anyone to do justice to anyone else. Here I met a few old acquaintances. In particular Tristan Tzara with his grey respectable dignified air which it is so difficult to associate with his dadaist and surrealist past. I had last met him in Spain. M. Julien Benda whom I had also last seen seven years previously in Madrid at the Writer's Congress, shuffled up to me walking in his peculiar way as though he always wears carpet slippers. He looked at me with his somewhat wicked air of a mocking old man, and said: "Have you read my article in *Confluence?*" Rather taken aback at this being his first question after all the years of bloodshed which had divided us, I said that I was afraid I had not done so. "It is an article of great importance," said M. Benda, "I put them all in their places and they will be very angry." With that he shuffled off and left me, while someone else explained that the purpose of the article was to attack nearly all his contemporaries, and, still more, the younger generation of writers for their treachery to Reason.

I felt that I had disappointed M. Benda, not that he cared very much. It was more disappointing for me personally to disappoint the kind and sympathetic M. Tzara which I did subsequently by writing an article in the Review *Horizon* in which I neglected the Maison des Intellectuels at Toulouse for the far less significant (according to M. Tzara) Cercle des Intellectuels at Montpelier (which M. Tzara describes as a "grotesque institution existing only in Mr. Spender's imagination"). Here is an opportunity to explain that in a certain sense this book is much nearer to being a romance than an official report. I am not trying to do justice to things in their order of importance, and if I chose to write ten pages about a maid servant rather than about a Commissaire of the Republic to me it would seem "grotesque" to accuse me of slighting the Commissaire of the Republic. My point of view is really that since I have my own pen, my own paper, my own ink and my own typewriter, I write about what interests me rather than about what ought to interest me. As a matter of fact, in this lies my only chance of interesting my reader. I might even invent a few "grotesques" if that suited my purpose. And it is no slight on anyone if he is omitted.

In the evening there was a dinner given by the Commissaire of the Republic, M. Pierre Bertaux. Bertaux struck me as being a most remarkable man, tall and dark, with a glance of dazzling intelligence. Besides being a Commissaire, he is a scholar, a Germanist, and he has written one of the best books on the poet Hoelderlin. He became Commissaire of Toulouse in succession to another writer, the poet Jean Cassou, who had been badly injured at the time of the Liberation.

Throughout the meal Bertaux talked brilliantly of poetry. He asked me whether I was willing, when circumstances permitted, to collect together a small group of English writers to meet a similar group of French writers, staying in some house in France, where we might discuss together our work and thought during the past years of war and discover what we had each learned from our experiences.

When I started speaking about Germany, Bertaux said, with much decision: "There is no German problem. There is only a European problem." His thought was, I think, that so long as the unification of Europe was postponed a so-called German problem would continue to be artificially stimulated and to preoccupy people, but that within a unified Europe Germany would cease to be a problem.

The next day I had lunch with him and his family in the beautiful house of the Commissariat. His father, also a very famous German scholar, with a face at once intellectually distinguished and lined with the expressive motionless lines of a peasant's face, was there, and his wife, daughter of Jules Supervielle, the poet, and his two little sons, to whom I gave some English threepenny bits. The lunch was simple but excellent, with excellent red wine. After lunch we went out into the garden, which resembled a public garden, being surrounded by the buildings of the Commissariat. It was a fine afternoon and we lay comfortably on deck-chairs. A bell struck and Bertaux, with his smile of a noble and intelligent animal, said: "I heard this bell at the same time every day when I was imprisoned not two hundred yards from here, throughout the Occupation. . . . What I wanted to tell you last night was that during the time of our imprisonment my fellow prisoners and I learned many things which had little to do with aims for which we had been fighting. We learned values which were not included in our political programme. For example, we learned a lot from hunger; a lot from solitude; a lot from our comradeship; and a lot from having to live a life of bareness and simplicity and for a cause which seemed hopelessly lost. We feel now that we should try to study the lessons of that life in which our defeat was our victory and our loss our gain; and that we should try to integrate the lessons of that time into the things which we shall stand for in the future. In Montpelier a circle has been formed to study these things. When you go to Montpelier, I want you to speak to Professor X—— who will tell you something of these things."

The next morning I left for Montpelier. At Toulouse they had been perturbed to hear of the conditions in which I had travelled from Paris and now a place in a First Class compartment was taken for me. However, after a few miles of travelling the coach developed a hot axle. There was a great deal of delay and then all the First Class passengers had to move into a Third Class carriage. As the train got to places on the coast, this became very crowded. The corridor was so packed that at one stop the people who were in the corridor protested against those who were on the platform crowding in. A woman who really fought her way into the train addressed her fellow-passengers thus,

French Interlude

shouting down the corridor: "It's been like this ever since the Liberation. Everyone's become selfish, out for himself. During the Occupation we all helped each other. Then you wouldn't have tried to push me out." One or two people attempted to answer her, a few others turned away with a show of indifference, but it was obvious that she was one of those indiscreet and unpopular people who says what is in everyone's heart.

Myself, I had to fight very hard to get my suitcase out of the train when I arrived at Montpelier, because even the slight walk up the corridor to the place where I had left it when the train was emptier, seemed a threat to the living space of the people who had squeezed themselves onto my suitcase, which they seemed to regard not as a suitcase belonging to anyone at all but as a seat provided for them by the railway company.

At Montpelier I was met by Professor X—— and two students. We went at once to a restaurant with tables on a verandah overlooking a river, where we lunched.

The lecture at Toulouse had been the least interesting part of the proceedings there, for the audience, I am sure, and for me also. I had an impression of a large dark hall with a gulf between the audience and the platform. I shouted hoarsely in bad French across the gulf without having the impression that anyone understood what I was saying on the other side. And in any case it sounded to me a mixture of mispronunciations, longueurs and banalities. Occasionally I found myself looking at Bertaux sitting in the second row with his amused and friendly yet nevertheless superior expression, and I felt sorry that I was wasting his time. But I felt that his intelligence was of a kind which could forgive me for doing so.

In Montpelier it was different because the audience was of young students, boys and girls, who were anxious to help me to make myself understood. The chairman was even more gen-

French Interlude

erous in his overestimate of my virtues and physical appearance than the chairman in Paris had been. But afterwards two of the students wrote me an anonymous letter saying that they wished me to understand that the students were more sincere and serious in welcoming an English visitor than the overstatements of my chairman might make me understand. I do not record this as a criticism of my chairman, who was acting in accordance with a convention of politeness, but because it was one of many examples in France of people straining to make a quite special effort to understand and make themselves understood by the English, which I experienced.

Professor X—— asked me whether I would speak to a circle of teachers, doctors, workers, professional men and women who were one of the group of the Centre de Connaissance of which Bertaux had spoken to me. This was a demand which I could hardly expect or be expected to fulfil, since I had prepared nothing to say and to speak impromptu seemed quite beyond me. So I said that I would gladly listen if they spoke to me. This was agreed to and, later in the evening, I was shown into a large sitting-room where I met about a dozen people, unassuming in appearance for the most part, but extremely serious. There were, I believe, a doctor, a lawyer, a farmer and a gardener among them, and also a Russian who had settled in Montpelier and who was a teacher in gymnastics. Professor X——, speaking for the Group to me, said that they consisted of people who had had many experiences during the past years, all of which had tended to teach them the value of a rule of life, a discipline, and personal relationship based on affection and good faith: these things were not included in the aims of political parties, and political workers, if they thought about them at all, tended to take them for granted or to assume that they would grow out of the other aims of the programme. Therefore, they were searching for something outside politics, as well as for political improvements.

After Professor X—— had spoken, I was asked to state my own views about these things.

Everyone waited, and I felt panic-stricken. The difficulty in speaking in French was so great that it drove nearly every thought out of my head. "Begin talking among yourselves, try and express my ideas for me," I said, "and then perhaps, in a few minutes, I shall be able to speak."

They were so patient, so anxious to show that they were interested not in how I spoke French but in what I had to say that I overcame my shyness and spoke with an eloquence which quite surprised me, though it probably only added to their difficulty in understanding what I was saying.

I said that I quite understood that we should have aims of being rather than of doing; and that this was not the programme of any of the political parties. I realized that the revolutionary parties concentrated almost entirely on the means of producing revolution and hardly even considered the ends of a revolutionary society, far less what the meaning and value of life would be for an individual living in a society where more and more benefits were being widely distributed. Really there was no reason for believing that if everyone became as well off as the middle classes are to-day life would have more value and significance than it had for the average middle-class man or woman, obsessed with material aims, to-day. So I agreed that the formulation of a way of life which could be pursued in a better kind of society was one of the greatest of contemporary needs.

Nevertheless—I went on—I didn't believe that the search after a way of life or after personal salvation or after Nirvana was more important than the social revolution. In fact I was suspicious of the search for any way of living which ignored the political and social tasks of our time and I even thought that to that extent the political revolutionaries who insisted on political tasks were better than the people who ignored them because they thought that politics ignored the life of the spirit.

At this point I became confused, not so much because my French was giving out (it most certainly was doing so) as that a painful conflict between the idea of a philosophy of calm and acceptance in which I could ignore the social system and at the same time the idea that nothing I did was worth while unless I undertook my share in crude, unsympathetic tasks outside and beyond me, started to split my mind as though with a chisel.

"Tell us what your own experience during the past years has been?" Professor X—— asked me gently.

"During the Spanish war, I joined the Communists because I thought that they were the only—really the only—party to act energetically on behalf of the Spanish Republic. But almost at once I realized that as far as I myself was concerned this was a mistake. I could not see the whole of reality through their spectacles of what was necessary for action—though I understood the point of those spectacles, which is to achieve the utmost magnification of tasks of revolutionary action, at the expense of everything else and of every other activity. Since then my aim has been to pursue what I think is my own work and to develop my own sense of values—but always without losing sight of the larger task. Also never to allow myself to be forced into a position of hypnotized opposition to the communists and to Russia."

It may seem and perhaps is a gross egotism that I remembered little of that meeting except what I myself said—apart from the taste of the cakes which we ate afterwards, which I remember well. But the effort of speaking without preparation

French Interlude

in a foreign language had the effect of thrusting my own words into the foreground of my consciousness and making the words of other people seemed remote and distant. However, I had a strong impression of their not sharing my point of view about the necessity of politics.

The next morning I called on Professor X—— who gave me a curious document. The first part of this emphasized the "presence" of France both in body and in spirit in the rest of the world. The "body" was the grandeur of France's physical achievement in history and in her art, architecture, etc. The "spirit" was expressed in the French Revolution which had inspired the rest of the world. At the same time, contemporary France was reproached for "profiting too indolently from a too glorious past" and for the guilt of being content with mediocrity. The next section dealt with the need of France for the outside world as a complementary and fertilizing agency: a need which could be recognized and accepted with humility but without any false sense of inferiority. After this the document, apart from some practicable and reasonable proposals about contacts abroad, became rather mystical and spoke much of the Universal, of the technique of Communication and of Silence.

All this interested and puzzled me.

At Montpelier I stayed with the Commissaire de la République. He behaved with the utmost generosity in putting me up, because only the day previously he had endured the most tragic personal loss in his family. He asked me to dine with him alone as this misfortune made it impossible to give a dinner party. He was most courteous and kind at dinner, speaking a great deal of public affairs, particularly with violence of the Black Market, which he said was all-prevailing so that even schoolchildren thought of nothing else.

On the following day I returned to Paris. This time really

in comfort, as I travelled for the first three hours First Class and then moved to a Sleeping Car. While I was sitting in the corner of the First Class compartment next to the corridor, the corridor was crowded with deportees in their dull-grey clothing. The one nearest me had a complexion burned to pale rust by exposure, bristly sandy hair and blue eyes. He talked vigorously, making all the time vigorous windmilling gestures of his powerful rather fleshy arms. He said to two of his companions, looking at me: "If we were Russians, we would throw those people out of their seats in the First Class compartment and occupy them ourselves, taking all their baggage as our own."

This made me feel an access of social guilt. Besides, it seemed rather a glorious thing to want to do, but I was on the wrong sides of the barricade. In order to have at least a foot in the proletarian camp, and to show that I was one of those bourgeois who are spoken of in the Communist Manifesto as "coming over to the other side" at the decisive moment of struggle, I went into the corridor and offered the red-haired man my seat, though not my baggage. At this he became very embarrassed and said: "No, Monsieur, you see how I am dressed, and, besides, I haven't washed for many days. I couldn't possibly sit in a First Class carriage with respectable people."

I persuaded one of his comrades to take my place, while I talked to this red-haired man who had something frank and free about his manner. I asked him where he had come from. "From Graz, in Austria." "When did you leave?" "Oh, four weeks ago. We have been travelling ever since."

His comrades crowded round us. He was evidently regarded as their spokesman. "How were you liberated?" I asked. At that they all laughed. *"Liberated!* We were *liberated* by the Russians. They occupied Graz, where we French were quite happy. We got on very well with the Austrians. They let us more or less run the place. But when the Russians came along they shut us all up for three weeks and took everything from us. They looted Graz and robbed everyone we knew there. After three weeks they released us and told us we could find our way back to France. We crossed the North of Italy to get there. There, in Milan, we found all the Italian workers were communists, longing to be liberated by their comrades. There is no fate we could wish them more heartily," he added grimly.

I said: "You realize that there's nothing very surprising about the Russians looting Graz? Our troops, the British, have looted in Northern Germany, the Americans and the French have all looted every part of Germany when they first came into it."

"Oh, no," he said, "our troops are disciplined forces, and so are all the other Allies. They are civilized beings, not savages. They don't do such things."

I protested. But it was of no use. He was not interested in and could not imagine any conditions except those which he had seen with his own eyes. He had been told that the Russians were angels and now he saw that they were human he thought that they were worse than anyone else. "If you don't believe what I say," he said, "ask any of my comrades on this train. We all come from Graz, and they will all tell you the same story."

He then spoke of France. "We are disgusted with what we see here. We don't feel that we want to have anything to do with it. We have been away from our home for four years, and now we don't believe that we belong to this France of people who are all out for themselves. The Germans had discipline and they were absolutely fair. Everything was orderly there. No one was selfish. We need a little of that discipline over here."

I asked him where he was going now. He said dully that he was going back to his home. He added: "I shall miss my

French Interlude

comrades though. *Ils etaient de bons gosses."* I noticed that all the time we were talking he did not take his eyes off his comrades for a moment. If they left him, and walked into the corridor of the next compartment, he said: "Excuse me, sir," and darted after them, returning a few moments later to resume our conversation.

8.

EVEN TO-DAY EVERY CIVILIZED NATION HAS ITS AUTHENTIC kings or princes of life who are a measure of its past and present values. A city is made glorious partly by its past beauty but also by the sense that there are at least a few inhabitants living in it who are representative of the whole sum of the city's significance, past and present. A city without its great men is like a royal palace over which the royal standard does not fly and whose windows are barren because the king is absent. A beautiful city with no contemporary generation of great men is only a monument of the past, haunted only by the present, and not lived in by it. A city in which the great men consist only of astute politicians and men of science, and which has no outstanding artists or thinkers, or with artists who devote their talents to flattering power, is a centre of barbarism. A city like Dublin, where all the great men have gone into exile, gives the impression of a deserted shrine. And tourism is the phenomenon of foreigners going to visit a place for the purpose of seeing its past greatness and not for the purpose of entering into its contemporary livingness. The Italian cities (and not th' Italian countryside which still has its peasants), having too fe great individuals who are the equals of the great Italians of '

French Interlude

past, breed tourists from within their own bodies, as a corpse breeds worms. Everyone who goes to them is a tourist because it is impossible to be anything else. It is impossible to have a relationship with the contemporary greatness of Italian cities which equals that of one's relationship with their past. The most cultivated Italians become tourists in their own country, sucking up their own past. And modern Italian literature, even in as great a writer as Leopardi, tends to become tourist or Guide Book literature, paying rhapsodic attentions to Italian monuments.

The magnificence of France is that one need not be a tourist there. There are contemporary lives which shine as the great lives of the past shone. And thus I feel myself not to be a tourist because I have spoken with the great living French writers and artists.

I climbed up the narrow staircase to Picasso's studio. At the top of the staircase and at the entrance to a room like a broad corridor which led to the studio, there were three or four of those beautiful and gentle pigeons with grey almost silken feathers, of which he has made several drawings in recent years. These drawings retain in his work the feeling of the Blue Period (there is a beautiful painting belonging to this epoch of a child holding a dove in his hand) and they flutter around his studio like messengers from the Epoque Bleue.

In this outer gallery I found Picasso talking to a man who had a picture under his arm. Picasso shook hands with me, we said a few words recalling our last meeting, which had been during the Spanish Civil War, and then he turned back to the man and said: "A charming water colour, but unfortunately not by me. What a pity."

He spoke French with the Catalan accent which is like a slight vibration running through his words. The man with the picture went. Then he turned to the rest of us and said: "You know, people are always bringing pictures up here, which are supposed to be by me. Most of them even have a forgery of my signature on them. I believe that there are laws which protect me against this kind of thing. Surely, I think I could take an action," he went on, with a certain naiveté as though the possibility had just occurred to him. He looked round, holding the question before him in his eyes as he seems to hold every expression in his gaze with a certain concreteness, as though his glance had the power to levitate a glass or a table.

On both occasions that I was with him in his studio, I wandered round looking at things while he talked with his friends. But all the time, while I pulled canvases out from behind other canvases, I was aware of him standing and talking to a group of people gathered round him, talking as though he were talking to friends in the street, in the open air, not making conversation, but occasionally throwing a question at someone, listening attentively to the reply and then not carrying on with the conversation, relapsing into silences not of withdrawal or of self-immersion, but more of a switching-off of his attention from listening to looking and being present.

Meanwhile, I was looking at the pictures. Amongst his own pictures there were other paintings, a Matisse flower-piece, and, if I remember rightly, a large reproduction of a painting by Matthias Gruenwald. But most of the paintings were, of course, his own. Still lifes, paintings of Paris, fantastically distorted heads, paintings of the patterns made by a tomato plant in a pot in front of the window. Some pictures had the glowing colours of stained glass windows fused together by lines as strong as leading, some were the colour of flesh and blood in the raw, or of bone exposed by the knife, some seemed to have absorbed into themselves the stone-grey stillness of the streets and courtyards of the Latin Quarter. It seems to me that the essential of his paintings is a simple statement, a gesture, a moment in which an image anchored in a visual experience is released into poetry. There are few of the paintings which do not seem to originate in something actually seen; often his distortions are not distortions of a reality which is not distorted but they are distortions seen in real objects, distorted visual experiences of a kind which most of us tend to eliminate from our visual consciousness, because we notice only what we see in a familiar, useful and "normal" way. For example, the two eyes appearing on one side of the face or one eye appearing directly above another or two faces merging into one face—and many other such apparent distortions—are derived from what we actually see when another face is pressed very close to one's own and one sees out of focus. Picasso's most distorted and—in a conventional sense—ugliest pictures of women often have a strange tenderness suggested by a distortion which is the development of an intimate kind of visual experience.

It has been said by many critics that Picasso is a poet of painting. This is true and it may be one reason why poets (for example, Paul Eluard and Jean Cocteau) love his work so passionately, but nevertheless he does not do what many poetic painters do—paint pictures of generalized poetic images. His pictures are of the moment when the experience is in process of becoming transformed into the poem. The anchor to the original experience is there, the cord which ties the balloon of the poem to the experience is there, and the balloon reaching into the stratosphere is there also. This gives the picture a sense not so much of release as of something being released. The tensions of freedom and of imprisonment, of body and spirit, of experience and of poetic transformation are all there at the same moment. And therefore they have the immediate quality of an exclamation, an utterance, a fragment of calligraphy, a protest and an acceptance.

To walk in the street with him, to enter a restaurant, is like being with a magnificent animal, the glow of whose gaze warms everything round him. In a restaurant, he will take up a piece of paper and start tearing it into a shape which is immediately interesting. I think it was Gertrude Stein who told me that with an old hat, or a piece of tin, he can hammer out a beautiful object. The reason for this is precisely his rootedness in things. He seems to see in every object its potentiality to become a symbol in his art. And his audacity, far greater than that of all his contemporaries, is that he does not turn an object such as a skull or a mandolin into a symbol in his art which has lost its relationship with real skulls or real mandolins but his art is the means by which real things assume, in infinite variety, a symbolic significance. At a certain period, he did many paintings in which there were mandolins. Other painters then assumed that there was something peculiarly significant about mandolins, or at any rate about the idea of a mandolin when expressed in the painting of Picasso, and they could think of no other object in nature more worthy of being transformed into their art than a mandolin. Mandolins became in their pictures conventional symbols for a certain poetic attitude towards art, which could not be replaced by anything else except mandolins. Then Picasso turned to skulls, to bird cages, to candles and candlesticks, to fruits and flowers, to tins and leaves, pots and pans—all the objects in his later pictures. It became evident that he could discover the symbolic aspect in everything.

At the restaurant, Picasso asked me about Germany. The conversation turned to the re-education of Germany. Picasso took up a piece of bread and said with a smile and a shrug of resignation: "Of course, I always say if everyone would paint, political re-education would not be necessary." I think he meant by this that painting puts people in a sane and healthy relationship to objects around them. He did not mean that he wanted the world flooded with bad pictures. He was talking really about an ideal—the extension of the attitude of the artist —and especially the painter—towards his art to the majority of people.

He said this seriously and yet with a realization that he was wishing the impossible.

A bookseller who had just been forced to give up his bookshop by the landlord, was at lunch with us. He complained that he would require a million francs to start a new bookshop and he said to Picasso: "I ask your advice because you know so much about business." Picasso made a great effort to enter into a business conversation about rents and so on but he then withdrew from the conversation as the bookseller raised one objection after another to all his suggestions. But the subject rather preoccupied Picasso throughout lunch. When we were leaving the restaurant he noticed an empty shop in the street and pointing to it triumphantly, he said: "There is the thing for you! Why don't you take that shop? It certainly wouldn't cost a million francs!"

The bookseller objected that it was in the "wrong" part of Paris.

"But this is the Latin Quarter. This is where everyone sells books, Sylvia Beach and Adrienne Monnier have bookshops only a few hundred yards away. Everyone would come here and buy your books and you would have a marvellous clientele."

"But the shop isn't large enough, and although it may be the Latin Quarter, this particular street isn't right."

At this Picasso said: "You want to sell books, don't you? If I wanted to sell books, I'd take a shop anywhere in order to sell them. And if I couldn't find a shop, I'd sit on the pavement and sell them. And people would buy them from me." He gave a vague gesture which showed the whole world and all the possibilities of doing anything one wants in it. Then he relapsed into a heavy silence. There was no answer to this.

9.

THERE IS PERHAPS LESS TO SAY ABOUT WELL-KNOWN WRITERS than about anyone else. For the truth is that good writers do really live in their works. The most interesting fact about them is the mere fact of their existence. Virginia Woolf shows a right instinct when she describes her hero Orlando looking into a room and catching a glimpse of a man seated at a table writing, with his back to Orlando: that is William Shakespeare. To-day when there is doubt about the whereabouts and the existence of many people in Europe, one notes that in Paris the French writers continue to exist. That Jean Paul Sartre sits every day for several hours in the Café Flore where he appears to be writing his books. That Aragon and his wife Ilse have a large book-lined flat, not so very far from Jean Cocteau's flat.

What amazes me about Aragon is his power of shedding his own past and living wholly and completely in his own present. He certainly has rather the air of a crusader, and his features, greying yet young and ardent, seem rejuvenated in his own eloquence. His armour is his absolutely invincible consistency with his own point of view at any given moment, which, of course, is also to-day the Communist Party point of view. To Aragon, the fact that there are people on this planet who still hold views which he, Aragon, held the day before yesterday—

surrealists, internationalists, etc.—seems strange and amusing, and he will comment on the existence of these ghosts of a past which he has disclaimed, with surprise. Another source of strength in his power of identifying himself with persons and causes which he supports. To mention three, he identifies himself with France, Ilse and the Communist Party. In short, Aragon is really a great force, before whom I feel a certain uncritical awe, because I am incapable of assuming an attitude of absolute confidence about anything.

When Aragon came to London at the end of the war, he walked around the streets and he wept when he saw the bomb damage and the extent to which London had suffered. I mention this fact, because he was accused by one of the English critics of insensibility towards the effort of England in the war, owing to the fact that he made a lecture in London in which he paid but scant tribute to the efforts of England. Aragon has sometimes been accused of discourtesy and vanity, but myself I have always found him most courteous. During the Spanish War, once when I passed through Paris I did not call on him because I thought he would be far too busy to see me. He reproached me next time we met with such warmth that afterwards I always made a point of telephoning him, and I always found that however busy he was he would arrange a meeting.

The flat of André Gide is on the fourth floor of a house in the Rue Vaneau. The whole flat, including the corridor, is lined with books. There is a waiting-room which is a reception-room not just for people but also for all the books by all M. Gide's contemporaries which arrive daily. Gide sits in his study, surrounded by books, photographs, paintings and many trophies, wearing an Arab cloak and a cap which resembles the long sleeve cap I have seen in the portraits of mediæval moneylenders. He is incredibly active for his age. He walks along the road reading a book held out opened in front of him. Under one arm he carries the most recent Reviews containing the work of the youngest writers and a new American novel. He misses nothing, observes everyone, diagnoses every relationship. He is not only observant but punctilious. In the course of conversation he gives me the telephone number of Albert Camus. I write this down on a piece of paper. Twenty minutes later he gives me the telephone number of Jean Schlumberger. While I am making a note of this, he says: "Please write it on the same piece of paper as that on which you wrote the telephone number of Camus. You will lose both numbers otherwise." He is interested in everything which concerns Germany and he wishes to go there himself to make his own observations. But there are complications, he does not wish to go officially and yet everything has to be arranged for him so it is difficult to go in any other way. He inquires closely about a friend in Germany. To illustrate the fact that this friend feels lonely and isolated I mention his complaining once or twice when I left after calling on him for two or three hours. Gide is astonished: "Three hours! But how could you possibly spend more than an hour with anyone!" Although this is not meant as a hint, I take good care to leave before an hour is up.

Thus all this life scattered all over Paris continues, a little shabbier, a little dustier, than before, often sick and ashamed of itself, but still very much alive. The buildings still stand, the gardens in the Palais Royal are still beautiful, though, as Jean Cocteau remarked to me when we walked through them: "The little toy cannon at one end of the garden which used to be fired every day at midday has been stopped ever since the real guns began to fire."

Journeys Through the British Zone

SEPTEMBER AND OCTOBER 1945

1. An Officers' Mess

THIS MESS IS SITUATED IN A SUBURB OF DUESSELDORF, ON THE shores of a small artificial lake near the Rhine. The Mess itself is a dull villa, but directly opposite it, on the farther side of the artificial lake, there is a baroque castle which looks like a setting for an opera of Mozart. It is torn by a huge gap in one side and has been partly gutted by fire. The remains of a charred fire engine hang over the large hole in its side, like a large long insect with withered spindle legs. The rest of the interior retains its charming unbroken ripeness. The castle is all of a pink colour which looks well and very absurd: a Dresden china shepherdess only partly broken in a city where nearly everything else is broken.

I arrived at about eight in the evening, after the officers had dined. They were drinking in the lounge, and the conversation was very bawdy. A Major, an officer with a square face above a strong jaw, bristly moustache, grizzled grey hair brushed back, took the lead in this conversation. He had the manner of a Preparatory Schoolmaster whose past is a fascinating mystery to all the boys. He showed me to my room and then to dinner. He invited me to join the other officers in going to a drinking Stube—an Officers' Club—at Duesseldorf. I accepted, and after

I had finished my dinner we went, in two cars. The conversation continued, as before.

The Weinstube was one of those German drinking cellars which resemble a chapel in a Gothic Cathedral. We sat at a table opposite a very elaborate tiled oven. The Major told me that he always sat there because he liked looking at the decorations on the tiles, which seemed to depict the Creation. He told me that he had been in India, and he advised me in my work, to treat the Germans as Indians. "Put one of them in a position of responsibility and say to him 'On thy head be it,' if those under him misbehave."

A young officer, Captain Royall, seemed to think that I was in a position to influence the political development of the Rhineland. He got extremely excited. "You ought to realize," he said, "that the Christian Democrat Party is a large-scale Catholic racket in Cologne. The whole administration is corrupt." "How do you mean corrupt?" "I mean that anyone can get a house on the outskirts of Cologne by bribing a member of the German administration with cigarettes." I said that I could scarcely believe that Adenauer, the Mayor, was not an honest man. "Adenauer is a wily old fox. Personally, he may be honest, but the rest of his administration is not, and he knows it." "Which party do you believe to be honest, then?" "The only honest people in Germany are the Social Democrats —and they are too honest to get anywhere." I asked him whether he thought that another administration could replace that of Adenauer in Cologne. "Don't you realize," he said, excitedly, "that thousands of people are going to die of cold and starvation this winter? It's an appalling situation. You ought to make them do something about it." "What?" I asked. "It would be a catastrophe if Adenauer fell," he shouted. I found all this rather complicated to follow so I pointed out to him that a moment ago he had been accusing the Adenauer administration of corruption. "I know," said Captain Royall, "but all the same, there should not be elections till the spring as this administration is the only one that can get through the winter, corrupt as it is. All the same, something ought to be done, you ought to see that something is done."

He did not stop telling me that something should be done throughout the evening.

When we left, everyone realized that the raw Rhine wine was very strong. I was driven home by the Major. He said: "Old boy, I have one rule on these occasions. I drive home extremely slowly. No one is going to rush me. I hope you won't object to my extreme circumspection." He drove very slowly down a blind alley. I suggested that it might be a good thing if I got out and directed him while he turned the car. "I may be a bit tipsy," he said, "but I am not accustomed to people showing a lack of confidence in my ability to back my own car." After this I said no more. He turned the car round successfully and then we crawled back, crossing from side to side of the road and going right over five or six traffic islands, until at last we got home. He made a special point of driving, still very slowly, right into the garage.

At lunch the next day, the Major told a story to illustrate the pedantry of German doctors. In 1929 he had had a serious operation at Leipzig. He was laid on the table and given an anæsthetic which did not make him unconscious because "it is well-known that people who drink rather more than other people take rather more than the average time to go under after an anæsthetic. So, while I was lying fully conscious on the table I saw the surgeon approach me, having wiped his knife on the sole of his foot. I said: 'Hi! What are you up to? I'm conscious.' The surgeon replied: 'You are *not* conscious. You have been given 33 c.c. of anæsthetic, which is exactly the quantity required to send a man of your height, weight and age into oblivion.' At this, as I was fighting drunk with the ether he had administered, I got off the table and assumed a posture of aggression. Thereupon, three nuns sat upon me. One held my left arm and the other my right arm, while a third sat on my feet. The surgeon then attacked me with his knife, and I fainted."

In the afternoon, I walked through the gardens of the Schloss down to the Rhine and took some photographs of sunken barges. A man who was fishing asked for a cigarette and then, as a reward to me for it, told me how much he preferred the English to the Americans who were *"richtige wilde Menschen."* He added that "all of us are guilty for the Nazis." I found myself wondering what sort of song the Rhine maidens are singing to the British soldiers stationed near the Lorelei.

In the evening I went to a concert given by the Symphony Orchestra of Duesseldorf. They played a Mozart Symphony and Beethoven's Pastoral Symphony, to an audience composed entirely of British soldiers. Nothing has made a sadder impression on me than this orchestra of pale, sick-looking elderly men, playing with great purety of tone but no energy or zest amongst the ruins of their city to the Army of Occupation. Such a scene suggests an eternal picture of a race driven into bondage. One flautist, in particular, was a pathetic old man, who played with a pure tone but a slight tremolo throughout.

On the following evening, the Colonel, who had been away for some days, returned to the Mess. His advent produced an atmosphere of respectful gloom. He had brought with him two very tough ducks, which we ate for dinner. None of us had a knife which would cut any part of the ducks, which made the meal even gloomier. The Colonel, tugging at his moustache, explained the ducks by saying: "Of course, I'm an absolutely lousy shot and I never hit anything, but when I was at Bunde, I went out shooting, and seeing a flight of duck come over I just let blaze with both my barrels and, to my amazement, two birds fell to the ground." This story was received in glum silence, as was everything the Colonel said. He had an air of saying everything in order to make an effect—which he never made.

Further specimen conversations at the Mess.

Colonel: "I observe, Major ——, that you have acquired a new mansion along the shores of the lake."

Major (who has been gazing gloomily at his plate): "Mansion, sir? What do you mean?"

Colonel: "I observe that you have a new property just along the road."

Major (grasping that a joke is coming): "To which of my many estates do you refer, sir?"

Colonel (smiling): "To the one entitled Surrey House. Surely, you live in Surrey, and I was right in concluding that this house is yours?"

Or:—

First Officer: "I saw your car this morning, Major."

Major: "Do you refer to the sky-blue Rolls Royce with the silver-plated bonnet?"

Etc., etc.

2. The Film Unit

ONE EVENING IN DUESSELDORF I MET AT THE OFFICERS' CLUB a man whom I had known slightly for some years, whom I shall call Boyman. When I had last met him, five years ago, he had been a surrealist painter. He was now a film photographer, and was occupied in making a film of Military Government in Germany. Since we last met, Boyman had acquired white hair and several lines on his forehead without his looking older, except that these signs were very noticeable in contrast to his perpetual youthful expression, so that all the time I was noticing that he was, in fact, older.

Boyman said he was working on a film of Military Government. The officers whom I was with all groaned and said: "My God, that's the end. A film of Mil. Gov., my God, my God."

Boyman talks an Anglo-American-Continental Film World slang in which he mixes up phrases such as "Oh boy, oh boy," with cockney such as "Bob's-your-uncle." He combines the gestures of a G.I. with those of a farouche type in a René Clair film. When he speaks French, he uses the conditional tense as often as possible in order that after the phrase *"si on faitça,"* or *"si on ne fait pas ça,"* he may introduce his favourite colloquialism, *"On est foutu."*

He told a story which was supposed to illustrate the irresponsibility of the Germans. He said that in Essen he had seen a woman go to a tap in the main street to get some water. The tap would not work. She turned to Boyman and said: *"Kaput."* Boyman pointed to another tap some yards away. *"Das ist auch kaput,"* the woman said. Then she shrugged her shoulders and looked all around her with an air of taking in the whole of Essen and said: *"Alles ist kaput."* Boyman said that it was "characteristic" of Germany to-day that she did not draw the moral that things were "kaput" through the fault of the Germans themselves.

Although I met a woman in Bad Oeynhausen who caused

me to make much the same reflection, this irritated me. I observed that if one was living from day to day in a cellar without water laid on and with very little food, one probably would not keep on moralizing all the time.

After this the conversation turned to the Press. Boyman, who was very excited about his own film, was utterly contemptuous of journalists and war correspondents, because they had not noticed anything that he had noticed. "Boy oh boy," he said, "What they miss, the dumb, daft, dolts that they are. For instance, not one of these idiots has had the sense to see that the best story since *Citizen Kane* is to be found in Villa Huegel, the house of the Krupps family, near Essen. Gee, what a scoop that would be if they could see beyond their champagne cocktails at the Mess! The Krupps family ate every day at a table to seat a hundred people with a table cloth which requires a special machine to wash it. Oh boy, oh boy, those marble halls!" He spread his hands out in a terrific Continental gesture of ecstasy, in which, with his long, large, thin features and very prominent eyes he looked oddly like a caricature of an El Greco saint.

I said that I had travelled home some weeks ago with a correspondent coming from Berlin who complained to me that he had many excellent stories which his paper refused to publish, about the desperate conditions in Berlin.

One of the officers at our table said that the worst paper in England and the most unscrupulous was the *Daily* ——, which we all agreed that we liked reading most. Then someone else remarked that oddly enough nearly all the journalists on this paper—which was conservative in politics—were socialists. I said: "We all find it difficult here to understand the unrepentant attitude of the Germans. We are astonished to find that everyone was so sincerely or cynically, a Nazi. And yet none of us is surprised to find that all the journalists on the *Daily* —— write in support of a policy which they do not believe in when they are not under the very slightest compulsion to do so. At least it may be said for the Germans that they were forced to be Nazis. But no one forces socialists to write up the politics of the *Daily* ——."

Boyman had not listened to the conversation. Now he interrupted it to describe a scene which he had been "shooting" at Cologne. He had been at work in the ruins of the Law Courts, when he became aware of an unpleasant smell of burning. On investigating, he found out that this was caused by several families living in the ruined cellars making fires on which to cook their meals from cheque books and old records of the Palace of Justice.

He talked a great deal more and said that the damned fool of a British public "had no realization of these conditions." His attitude that everyone except his Film Unit is a bloody fool, annoys me. Besides which, why should the British public be sensitive to conditions in Germany? I often wonder whether sensibility is such a virtue as I myself am inclined to suppose it to be, since my own experience is that being sensitive, aware and imaginative does not prevent one from being selfish. In fact, it makes one egocentric. All the same, Boyman is a live wire, and part of my irritation with him is undoubtedly due to jealousy and competitiveness. After the evening with Boyman I went to bed doubly depressed: by the squalid destruction of Duesseldorf and by the assertive cocksureness of Boyman.

3. My Driver

My driver is young, communicative and helpful. When we set out in the large smart Humber which was allotted to me at Bunde, almost his first remark as we got on to the dull broad grey ribbon of Hitler's autobahn was: "Is there any loot which you would like me to get you, sir?" I refused this offer, but went on talking to him throughout the journey to the Ruhr and thence to Duesseldorf. He thought that not the least of Hitler's crimes was the construction of the autobahn "which is so boring that unless you talk to someone you go to sleep driving along it." This was quite true, I found. The autobahn has the capacity to turn every landscape into one huge ribbon of wide grey expanse. He also complained that "they had never made up their minds what material to make the autobahn of, some of it being of asphalt, some of concrete, and some of various other materials."

He explained to me that he was new to the R.A.S.C. and would like to take very great care of the Humber, as his reputation rested on this trip. He asked me hopefully whether we were likely to be going to Brussels. I had to disappoint him. He told me that he came from a town in Kent, that his girl friend had swiped his camera and that he did not believe in "woman's intuition," because when he went out every other night with a different girl and explained to his real girl that he spent these alternate nights with his mother, she believed him. He said that the English A.T.S. girls were jealous because the soldiers all went with German girls but this served them right because in France they themselves had always gone with Canadians and Americans.

I asked him why the German girls are supposed to be preferable to the English ones. His answer was very utilitarian, in fact the so-called Utilitarians would have been perturbed in their philosophy of "the greatest pleasure being the greatest good" by it. He explained that the English girls expected to be taken out and given a good time. The German girls on the other hand, were good for a night's fun, cost nothing, and you did not have to see them again. I asked him what happened if the German girl liked you and wanted to see you again. He said dryly, "that would be just too bad for the German girl."

The Ruhr is the most dramatic kind of industrial country. The towns are not so large but that one has always a clear picture in one's mind of the surrounding fields and patches of countryside between them. Indeed, the countryside near the Ruhr has a character of its own, of bright emerald gaps surrounded by the hard towns with their skeleton-like silhouettes of pit-heads and chimneys and their massive factories a gelatinous colour in the ice-clear light of that part of Germany. There are always people walking in the fields and along the roads between these towns. They have the air of scraps of paper, bits of rag, being blown from one town to another. There are sunflowers sometimes in the fields or in gardens at the edges of the towns. One has magnificent glimpses of the tall thick wheels of petals against the ghostly background of crouching factories and slums. Altogether the Ruhr contains all the poetry of the modern cinema—the poignant contrast between urban and rural life.

This sleek, green, fat countryside with the towns spreading all over it and with factories often between the towns, reminds me of a sow's belly with udders leading to subterranean richness; a belly covered with parasites armed with suckers, shovels, proboscises, tubes feeding upon it in an unnatural way. A factory with its pitshaft or its diagonal line of shovels and trucks lifted to plunge into the earth, looks like nothing more than a disgusting parasite which has settled upon a luxuriant living flesh.

The Ruhr is now, of course, a mass of ruins, though it is difficult to kill parasites, and many factories still have smoke pouring from their chimneys. It seemed miraculous that the car survived the journey through the Ruhr towns. On either side of the roads there were heaps of ruins, and the roads themselves were almost impassable, often being covered with glass and rubble. Ends of tramlines, curled up like celery stalks, protruded from holes in the streets. All these towns are utterly broken. We had a small meal in the surviving hotel in the centre of Essen, which is used as a Transit Mess.

Thus we got safely to Duesseldorf. The morning after my adventures in returning home from the Weinstube, I mentioned to my driver that I had hunted for him the previous evening. One of the officers at the Mess had suggested taking my car for the evening. My driver said: "I would have driven it for him, sir, if you'd wanted me, but not let him drive it, as those officers are chronic drivers who would wreck any bloody vehicle."

After a week we left Duesseldorf for Bonn, which I proposed to make, for a few days, the centre of my work. On the way to Bonn, my driver told me about his hobby which is making model petrol engines. He told me that he and his "mate" at home have done this for years. Their specialty is model speed boats, but they have also made model cars and even a model dredger. He talked happily of all the technicalities of these models until I was hypnotized into a kind of dream.

When we were passing through Cologne, he remarked, looking at the ruins, "One gets pretty callous when one's seen people blown to bits in front of one's eyes every few minutes. After Normandy, the only thing that really upset me was running over a kid. I couldn't help it, sir. She ran out into the road right under my wheels."

He told me that his father was a chauffeur and that he himself had driven a car from Brighton to London when he was ten.

Outside Bonn the car developed trouble. We went to a garage where an engineer tinkered at the engine from eleven until three in the afternoon. He looked at the plugs, the carburettor, the ignition, and finally he took out the pump and put in a new one. Nothing prevented the car spitting and backfiring. He decided finally that the trouble must be the carburettor but there was no other carburettor suitable for a Humber in the garage. So he sent out various of his hands to search surrounding garages for a suitable carburettor.

I was astonished at the devotion of this man to his job, which prevented himself and both of us from getting any lunch. All the time he and his companions carried on a conversation half in mechanical half in biological terms about the engine. This is a special language and people who tinker about with machinery all day live in a special world, perhaps even more self-contained than that of pure scientists, because it is more complete. Pure science must obviously to some extent be a rejection of the world of everyday life, but these men have integrated their everyday life into their feeling of machinery, and they pay a broken-down car which comes into the garage considerably more attention than is paid to most patients who come into most hospitals. Their minds have grasped a very complex and elaborate ritual of machinery.

I thanked the engineer for spending so much time on the car. He said: "This time last year we was often working twenty hours out of twenty-four." "Yes, and lucky if we could sleep those four hours in a ditch," said my driver.

We got to the Officers' Transit Mess at Bonn at 3.15 P.M., leaving the car, as the engineer had decided, besides looking for a new carburettor, to experiment with the valves.

4. Libraries

THIS, MY SECOND VISIT TO GERMANY, WAS FOR THE PURPOSE of opening libraries in the Ruhr and the Rhineland. Owing to the fact that the libraries, together with their staffs, were supposed to be completely nazified, they had all been closed since the beginning of the Occupation. The authorities had now decided that the coming winter was going to be very hard, so it would be a good thing to get the libraries open as soon as possible, so as to provide the Germans with something else to think about during the following months, than their living conditions. I was supposed to carry out a policy of "purging" the libraries of the Nazi members of their staffs, and also of their Nazi literature. We did not wish the Nazi books to be destroyed, but we wished them to be taken out of the libraries and put aside in a separate room, under lock and key.

The German library system is very complicated, and I never fully grasped it, as, owing to the fact that my car was nearly always broken down, I was not able to carry out my work and my inquiries into libraries at all satisfactorily. Also I lost interest in it rather soon. However, there are several kinds of libraries in nearly every German town, and it cannot be assumed that the official Town Public Library is necessarily as important as some large lending library run by some other organization than the State. For example, in Bonn the important library is a Catholic Library called the *Borromaeus Library*, and the *Volksbibliothek* is of little importance. The Catholic libraries, associated with their headquarters at Bonn, have many branches throughout the Rhineland. They are general lending libraries, doubtless with a penchant towards piety, but by no means devoted exclusively to religious works.

The routine of my library job was that I should first approach the Military Government authorities in each town, then the Oberburgermeister, and then the library itself. It was also necessary, of course, to make myself agreeable to the Military, as they could help me in many ways. In short, I had to pay my attentions to all local divinities, civilian, military, and even German.

The H.Q. of Military Government at Duesseldorf is housed in a huge modern red brick rectangular building built in several blocks round three-quarters of a square. Inside are very fine stone floors and staircases, with walls panelled with polished synthetic bistre-coloured stone, chromium rods and fittings, office furniture of polished walnut. Even the lavatories, with urinals of grey fine-grained marble, were worthy to receive the excretions of the highest Nazi officials.

I called at once on an English officer whom I had been told to see, a man with well-combed beautifully parted hair of a most presentable boy of fifteen, except that it had gone white. He had a cherubic complexion.

This officer was most friendly and helpful, as, indeed, was every officer I ever had to ask anything of in Germany. He seemed pleased that I was opening libraries, and he at once summoned the Mayor and the two chief librarians to his office. Before the Mayor arrived, he said: "When the Mayor comes in, don't shake hands with him or stand up. I don't believe in being friendly with them."

I was a little taken aback by this, because, presumably, the Mayor was an anti-Nazi, in which case there seemed to be no reason for not shaking hands with him. But the more one travels in the Zone the more one realizes that this distinction does not count. Whether one shakes hands or not with Germans is not even a matter of principle, it is a matter of feeling. And since this is so, perhaps officers who have fought the Germans are right not to shake hands with them if they do not wish to do so. Myself I was always polite to everyone, but then I had no strong reason for being rude.

The Mayor, having arrived, gave us his opinion about Dr. Peters and Dr. Reuter, librarians respectively of the *Volksbibliothek* and the *Landes und Stadt Bibliothek*. He said that Dr. Peters was no Nazi, although he had been a member of the Party. He did not think we need throw him out.

He said that Dr. Reuter was an old and honourable man whose reputation was above suspicion.

He said that about 60,000 books had been burnt in the libraries of Duesseldorf, and he added that the libraries had been or were in course of being purged.

Dr. Reuter then called, and I took him in the Humber to his library, whither he directed my driver. Dr. Reuter is one of those thin, elderly, spectral-looking Germans of an uncharming thin-lipped, pinch-nosed, leaden-eyed, sallow-skinned, scraggy-necked appearance, who yet have something vaguely dignified about them and a certain kindness and humorousness behind their steel-rimmed spectacles. They are like ghosts of a more romantic Germany of poets and philosophers. He wore an old mackintosh which hung on his body as though it were a clothes-hanger. His ears were stuffed with cotton wool.

His library—the *Landes und Stadt Bibliothek*—was, he explained, a scientific library used for the purpose of study. He explained frankly that it contained many Nazi books and he pointed out that it was extremely difficult to disentangle the Nazi from the non-Nazi works in various learned periodicals, which during the last ten years had presented a strange mixture of articles of real learning and valueless propaganda. He said that no one had access to the shelves of his library except the librarians, and that he had the most complete confidence in his staff. Therefore, he went on firmly, the Nazi books should be left where they were, though he was agreed that they should only be obtained by readers under special conditions, such as authorization from Military Government.

He said that the library would not be opened until the roof was repaired, and he asked if I could help in this (of course I could not). He emphasized that if the Faculty of Medicine at the University were reopened, it would be necessary also to open this scientific library. He showed me over the library, much of which was dripping with water, the roof having been completely destroyed. Water poured right through the whole building down even to books in the cellars. He took me to a little room, removed from the main library, where there were a bust of Heine and many of Heine's manuscripts, which he had preserved throughout the Nazi régime. The pale marble bust in a small dark room with empty shelves had a death-bed atmosphere which was a very suitable setting for Heine. He showed me also the last letter written by Heine to his mother in 1855.

Dr. Reuter then took me back to the main library which was his office, and he made a little speech. He said that just as he had preserved Jewish books during the Nazi régime, so now he thought it necessary to preserve Nazi books as they were of historical interest and, also, they were the most valuable weapon, in the long run, against the Nazis.

Fortunately I did not have to object to Dr. Reuter's position. We had no intention of destroying any books, but only of withdrawing the Nazi literature from circulation in the public libraries on the open shelves. However, my conversation with Dr. Reuter made me realize that there was little point in our policy. Anyone who wished to obtain Nazi books in Germany could easily do so, and to withdraw the Nazi books seemed only a piece of window-dressing which would give us a reputation for treating literature in the same way as the Nazis themselves had done. Indeed, the librarians who were closest to the Nazi policy were the quickest to understand and interpret our aims in the most far-reaching way. For example, a librarian in Aachen, said to me, to show how quick she was to understand: "Please, don't trouble, Mr. Spender. We understand exactly what you want, and there is no difficulty whatever about carrying out your instructions. You see, throughout the Nazi régime, we kept all the books by Jewish and socialist writers in a special cellar, under lock and key, as having only historical and scientific interest. All we have to do now is to take out these books and put them on our open shelves, while at the same time we lock up all the Nazi books, because now *they* only have historical and scientific interest."

There was this much to be said for our policy. The German libraries were flooded with Nazi books, the total effect of which had been to discourage the reading habit amongst Germans, because, even for Nazis, Nazi literature is almost unreadable. These books had to be got rid of somehow, and the libraries had to be built up again from what remained when the Nazi books had been taken away. Without a purge of the Nazi books, we could not really know where we were.

Dr. Peters was very different from Dr. Reuter. He was a tough confident-looking man with iron-grey hair, strong, scarred features. As soon as I was alone with him, he launched forth on a long defence of himself explaining that he had used his position (which as head of the *Volksbuecherei* of Duesseldorf he could only retain as a member of the Nazi Party) in order to combat Nazi efforts to nazify the libraries. He had been criticized by the Nazis on several occasions and there had been efforts to remove him from his post. He said that he was never on good terms with the Party and that he had almost been imprisoned by the Gestapo. He showed me a deposition stating all this with the names of several witnesses who would testify for him.

Besides this self-defence, he had that astonishing grasp of the principles of repression which seem to make the German officials always go further than is required in any direction which the Occupying Powers suggest to them. He had written an essay on the Evil of Nazi Influence in the State Libraries. This analysed the nazification of German literature under about eleven headings. He and his staff had put aside all the books in the library which came under these headings and were now reading and analysing them in order to make a complete report for the British Authorities. He calculated that it would take three or four months even to read through this great mass of unread propaganda. It was somewhat amusing to reflect that the effect of the policy I was representing was to make a lot of Germans read hundreds of Nazi books which no one had opened throughout the Hitler régime. But Dr. Reuter would probably have said, with that sudden contraction of his eyes behind his spectacles which was not exactly a smile, that this was a suitable cure for them.

I left it to the Civilian Military Government to decide

whether or not Dr. Peters should be retained. He had been a member of the Nazi Party, but he had also been head of this library for a great many years. Perhaps I should be ashamed of the fact that I took no pleasure in the thought that he might have to be removed. The reader who thinks as I did when I first came to Germany that the task of the de-nazification is simple, will have some grasp of the complexities in this account of the comparatively straightforward question of Dr. Peters.

In practice, I found that the libraries of the Ruhr and the Rhineland were capable of opening themselves without my intervention. In many cases, such as Bochum and Dortmund, the Military Government officers had had the good sense to open them already without any encouragement from me. In other places, such as the *Borromaeus Libraries* connected with Bonn, the libraries were really in control of priests who had always resisted Nazi influence. In every case, the Germans had automatically set about purging their libraries on the day of their towns being occupied by the Allies, if not before that.

5. Bonn

THE TROUBLE WITH MY CAR KEPT ME SEVERAL DAYS IN Bonn. I thought it was better to stay here, as I knew the officers and there was more chance of their helping me with transport here than in Duesseldorf. I went to see the Major in charge of Bonn during the absence of the Commanding Officer. He is a Yorkshireman; hard, strong, kind, sympathetic and egoistic. Yorkshire men are odd: they seem tough and full of bonhomie, and at the same time they have a streak of hypersensitivity in their make-up (or am I misjudging them by J. B.

Priestley?). The Major welcomed me and after listening to my various problems he explained the previous instructions he had received regarding libraries. I then mentioned nervously that my car had broken down. He could not contain himself when I said this. Producing a wad of papers from his desk he proved to me that he had at Bonn four cars for eight officers—an impossible situation. He said: "I needn't be in this job and I reckon that if I were at home I could be earning two thousand a year. However, I'm staying here because I think there is work to be done." All his nature, his opinion of himself, his opinion of the authorities and his own genuine goodness—were in the tone of voice in which he said these two sentences. Then he took up the telephone and arranged that I could draw one of the cars for the use of civilians, from the Civilian Car Pool.

As I was delayed at Bonn I called at the hospital to find out what had happened to Rudi Bach. They told me that he had made a very complete recovery and that he was living in a village between Cologne and Bonn, with his parents. So on the next occasion when I had to take a car to Cologne, I called at this village and looked him up. My reason for doing this was that I was beginning in my life to pay the penalty of writing a Journal. I was conscious that my only motive for seeing Rudi was to write up the sequel to the story of the penicillin which he had been given in July. My actions are now dictated partly by the desire of my Journal to achieve its own investigations through the agency of me, partly by the whims of my motor car and the intrigues of my driver.

It was quite difficult finding Rudi Bach, as his parents had informed the hospital authorities that his father was Mayor of the village where he lived. This, in fact, was a post which he had held many years ago, and at the Town Hall they knew nothing about a Buergermeister Bach. However, eventually I did find my way into the drawing-room of the Bach family, who were sitting round a table eating a large tea consisting mostly of some very good fruit tarts (directly you get even a few miles outside towns into the country you find that there is plenty of food).

Rudi Bach had made a sensational recovery. Instead of the thin dying boy of the hospital, I saw someone who looked like the Fat Boy in *Pickwick Papers*. He was really incredibly fat, with bulging cheeks, bulging thighs and a complexion like a suet pudding. The change was so marked that it was difficult in a way not to regret it, and in so far as I had been responsible for a miracle I reflected that probably all the Great Healers must have felt pangs of conscience when they saw the people they had healed fully recovered. I commented on his changed appearance, and Rudi Bach said airily: "Oh, this is nothing, I shall soon be much fatter. I am not properly well yet; only convalescent." He then proceeded to give me a lecture on the muscles of his heart, the moral of which was that he must rest a great deal, eat a great deal, do no work and *"sich richtig erholen."* He thought that he might do a very little sport in a few months time.

Frau Bach talked so much that I was not able to say much to the Fat Boy, for which I was fairly grateful. She was full of village gossip about the Nazis. She said that there was a lot of "underground" Nazi talk still going on and that the Nazis often still retained their powerful positions. She complained that rich Nazis who had fled from the Rhineland could now return and take possession of their houses, whilst the houses of non-Nazis were requisitioned. She said that she didn't believe in vindictive methods, because she was a Christian, but she did think that the Nazis might be compelled to do rough work in reconstructing Germany and that they might be the first to have their houses requisitioned. Also, they should not hold official positions. Some of the worst Nazis have been clever enough to avoid being Party members, but everyone knew who these were.

I pointed out that only a few days previously forty industrialists had been arrested in the Ruhr, and I said that perhaps this showed that the Nazis who still went around were not altogether secure.

Frau Bach was the most unctuous type of respectable pious hausfrau. She kept on impressing on me how godly and virtuous she and all her family were. She thought that all entertainments in Germany should be *serious* and she sincerely hoped that in future no one would be allowed to enjoy himself. She was afraid, she said, that already there were signs that people were beginning to do so. I told her not to worry and that I thought happiness was not one of Europe's worst troubles to-day. She protested that the entertainments in Germany to-day were not serious enough. She had seen posters in Bonn advertising cabarets. "The least one would expect, after all that the Germans have done, is that they should be compelled to have good music, good books, good theatre; nothing but what is good," she said severely, "Mozart, Beethoven, Goethe. Nothing else should be allowed."

When I got back to Bonn, my driver appeared in my room, his hands and some of his face smeared with oil, his cap on the back of his head, and a rueful troubled expression on his face. He said the car was still in the workshop. They said the fault lay in the ignition now, and this meant getting spare parts. The car went, but if we used it as it was now we would probably have trouble again in three or four days.

I stayed on in Bonn, taking advantage of such transport as I could beg from Transport Officers. A Transport Officer told me that in the garage three of the German workers were ill through undernourishment. He said that if he could do so he provided his workers with food that he got himself, because he simply could not maintain efficiency in any other way.

Jim Raven said much the same thing. The rations for a week for a German consisted of about a dessert-spoonful of some kind of fat, four pounds of bread, two thin slices of meat, the size of a crown piece each, if he was lucky, and, also if he was lucky, once a month, about half a pound of substitute tea or coffee. Formerly people had filled out this diet to some extent with potatoes, but during recent weeks potatoes had been almost unobtainable.

People with money get a bit more by going out into the country and scrounging round for what they can buy from peasants, or appealing to the generosity of friends.

During these days of my car being broken down, I was often left with little to do but observe conditions and listen to rumours. Some of the rumours had a tendentiousness which scarcely needs underlining. For example, the atom bomb produced one rumour that if the war had gone on for another week, Hitler would have used the atom bomb which the Germans had in readiness. This rumour sometimes took the form of: After all, Hitler was a good man. He had the atom bomb but he was too humane to let it be used. There are always many rumours in the hotel, among the waiters, to the effect that the Rhineland is either about to become part of the French Zone or else an Independent Republic.

The University of Bonn is to be opened in November. One afternoon I went to see two professors who discussed the curriculum for the coming Semester. They are obliged to limit their curriculum to the available books. It is very curious to hear them talk about books that have appeared in England and France during the past five years. It is like hearing people discuss events which may or may not have happened in another world. Such conversations take one back hundreds of years to a time when events that happened in other countries had an air of mystery and speculation about them. Nothing made me realize more how completely Germany has been cut off from the rest of civilization more than this conversation.

One day I went to see the chief sight of Bonn, Beethoven's birthplace. This is a few rooms of a pleasant house with a nice courtyard. Beethoven was born in a small room which is almost entirely filled by a very large bust, so large in fact that if the whole of Beethoven were modelled to the same scale there would be no room for him in the humble bedroom where his mother bore him. This seems symbolic of the inflatedness of great reputations.

The Beethoven Museum is very boring. There are dozens of very bad portraits of him or copies of very bad portraits and sculptures collected from all over the world. It is difficult to think of any artist who has inspired so many other artists to produce such bad works of art as Beethoven.

Beethoven's ear trumpets, which I remembered as a great feature of the Beethoven Museum before the war, have now been hidden in the "Beethoven Treasure" as they were considered too precious to risk losing.

The Beethoven manuscripts show a most astonishing variety of calligraphy. Beethoven really infused something of the spirit of the work which he created into the actual handwriting of each different work. For instance the curved markings over the figures of the Leonora Overture have a great freedom, like a freehand drawing. Beethoven's handwriting is not unlike that of Picasso. The MS. of the opus III Sonata has an abstract intensity and a great sense of concentrated movement. One can admire it as a drawing. I would like Picasso to see it.

6. Jung's Interview

ONE DAY I READ IN "AUSBLICK," A DIGEST OF ARTICLES FROM foreign periodicals published in Germany, an interesting interview with Professor C. G. Jung.

In this interview Jung says that all the Germans share a collective guilt for the crimes of the Nazis, whether they were Nazis, members of the army, anti-Nazis, or even refugees. The reason for this is, he says, that the whole German people and their leaders were "demoniacally possessed." Jung claims that the inner mentality and dream-life of anti-Nazis in Switzerland whom he has psycho-analysed show that they were as much "possessed" as the Nazis themselves. "Ten per cent of the German people are incurable psychopaths." "All the accusations of soullessness, bestiality, etc. which German propaganda made against the Russians, are descriptions of the Germans themselves." "It is no chance that the German chief of propaganda, Goebbels, should be singled out by having a club foot—that ancient sign of the demoniacally possessed man."

Jung goes on to argue that the only cure for German guilt is acceptance of it. *"Mea culpa, mea maxima culpa."* Therefore he thinks that the American policy of forcing Germans to visit concentration camps and witness the conditions which took place there, is wise. However, moral sermons to the Germans are not enough. Penitence cannot be imposed from without, it must arise from within. Jung hopes that prophets may arise in Germany who will preach penitence "because a people that can fall so deep must also be able to rise to great heights." He says that the German crimes are conditioned by a collective form of society, and that there is danger now of the victors using the methods of collectivization which are the most favourable medium for the activities of the demon. The English are saved from this danger by their strong sense of individuality, the Swiss by the fact that they are a small nation. The agents of the demon are the methods of mass suggestion of the Press, Radio and Film. The only way to overcome the demoniac forces is by communication between man and man.

This interview interests me greatly. I think that it is true though I don't know quite how to interpret the idea of demoniac possession. Perhaps it is not necessary to interpret it: it convinces, even if it is difficult to express in any other way. In a way, Jung does not go far enough in condemning only the German people. If all Germans are guilty whether or not they are Nazis and even if they live abroad, then how can he exclude other groups together with their opponents, Fascists, anti-Fascists, Cagoulards, communists, etc, in countries outside Germany? Also, can one judge German anti-Fascists by neurotic refugees treated in Switzerland who go to Dr. Jung for a treatment?

Actually, it would do little harm and might do a lot of good if everyone all over the world examined his or her conscience and seriously asked himself whether he was in any degree indirectly responsible for Nazism and all its consequences.

If such a self-examination were made, I think that a few Germans—some socialists and communists, some Catholics, some intellectuals, some scholars—would be as guiltless of creating the Nazi régime as anyone else in the world. At the same time, I agree with Jung that there is a special kind of German suggestibility—willingness to obey orders, thinking in generalizations, the search for panaceas, faith in power, which made many Germans capable of falling to deeper depths than many people of other nations.

The Occupying Powers are now—as Jung points out—prone to the very temptations which led to the downfall of Germany. Jung seems to think that the greatest dangers are collectivization, mass propaganda, the acceptance of mass ideas, the refusal to regard individuals as individuals. This last danger—or refusing to treat individuals as such—Jung himself seems not entirely to avoid, when he labels every individual German with collective guilt. The British—despite their respect for individuals—are rulers of an Empire, and it is here that their danger lies. Directly they go abroad they start generalizing about "the natives." This tendency towards facile generalization is surely shown in the extreme reluctance to distinguish between anti-Nazis and Nazis, or at all events between anti-Nazis and other Germans. The officers, far more than the rank and file, refuse to recognize that every German is a separate human being. They refuse to see that we must treat the Germans on a relationship of man to man and not of man to Guilty Beast. It may be objected that there are very few exceptional Germans. If this is so, then it should be at least possible to single them out and thus prove that we can treat the very few differently from the very many.

Often when Germans complain to me about conditions, I feel like making one of the stock replies such as: "Well, you lost the war, didn't you?" or "How can you complain when you belong to a guilty race?" However, these replies are not really the clever appeals to reality which some officers imagine them to be. They are simply crude applications of the formula that we refuse to regard Germans as individuals, to some particular individual complaining German. When you are face to face with an individual German (*any* individual German) the question of the extent to which he, as an individual, is responsible and guilty for the crimes of the Nazi régime, becomes a relevant one; to refuse to take it into consideration is simply an injustice, a refusal to consider the most relevant issue. To say to some particular German, who may be an anti-Nazi: "You are a German, I refuse to shake hands with you because, like all other Germans, you are guilty, and I am therefore going to requisition your house," is equivalent to saying: "I am victor and you are conquered. I regard your late government as guilty for starting the war and for many bestialities resulting from it and therefore I am going to exercise my privilege of ignoring your claims to be treated as a separate person with a separate body and soul and a separate personal history. I am going to ignore you as a human existence and treat you as a particle of a mass of collective guilt."

A few nights after the one on which I read Jung's interview, I was kept awake by a mosquito and I spent the time thinking about the question of German guilt. It is curious that since 1918 German guilt has been the only religious question, more than a mere external form, with which modern politics has been deeply concerned. It has been discussed with a great deal of obtuseness always. The arguments produced to prove that all Germans are guilty usually prove to most Germans (and to many thinking people everywhere) that they are not. For example, atrocities in Belgium in 1914, and atrocities in concentration camps in the recent war are crimes that most Germans know less about than is known by people in the world outside Germany, just as the educated British are the most ignorant educated public in the world as regards conditions in India.

The most important issues are (1) the political responsibility of the Germans in bringing Hitlerism into power, after

Hitler in *Mein Kampf*, Goebbels in many books and articles, and many other writers on the Nazi side, had made quite evident not only the aims but also the nature of the Nazi methods and Movement. (2) The orgiastic enthusiasm, false idealism, blindness and self-deception of the first years of Nazi power. The years 1933-35 are a period of which many Germans are still proud. They call it the period when the Movement was "idealistic." (3) The hardness of heart, baseness, corruption, indifference to the fate of the Jews and of many others during the whole history of Nazism. (4) The general degradation in every branch of spiritual and intellectual life accepted quite willingly by most Germans.

These points can all be argued about, but they contain the main features of German collective guilt. It can be seen too from them, that German guilt spreads beyond Germany. For example, how many of us to-day are guilty of the hardness of heart and indifference to the fate of others which condoned Nazism.

Another consideration is: "Towards whom were the Germans guilty?" At present the argument of guilt is used to assert the moral superiority of the Allies, and to justify all sorts of malpractices by them. There may be some "rough justice" in this, and there is certainly an inevitability about it which one has to allow for, but at the same time our brutality should not be justified by our moral superiority. If one considers that every German is guilty towards every allied soldier who wants to take his camera or his watch one confuses the issue. The Germans, if they were guilty, were guilty firstly towards their millions of victims and secondly towards themselves. Their most enduring crimes, from the consequences of which we must undoubtedly save them if we are to save Europe, were those of self-degradation.

Then the question of the guilt of the rest of the world must be considered. The conception of guilt cannot be isolated. Everyone is to some extent guilty for the crimes of everyone else, because everyone is to some extent responsible for the conditions which produce those crimes. Society uses murderers as instruments through which it commits what are really society's own murders. There is guilt of the German people, and every German has a certain relation or responsibility for that guilt. That is the sense in which the phrase "Collective Guilt" is true. It does not mean that every German is equally guilty but that every German should be conscious of guilt. Nor does German guilt give the Allies an automatic moral ascendancy, a kind of credit which gives them leave to behave as they like in Germany until such time as they decide that it is necessary to stop doing so in order to avoid becoming as guilty as the Germans. My neighbour's crime may make him worse than me but it does not make me better than him. On the contrary, while making him worse it may make me worse as well.

7. Joachim Bender

I MET IN COLOGNE A SCHOLAR OF DISTINCTION WHOM I SHALL here call Joachim Bender. Aged about thirty, extremely thin, tall, with long hands with very tapered fingers and a meek yet keen expression in his eyes, Bender works in a business house in Cologne. That is to say, he works in the cellar and ground floor of this great undertaking, of which everything else has been destroyed. As there is very little business, he has not much to do, and he is able to pursue his study of languages during his office hours.

Bender told me that, as a member of the Protestant community in Cologne, he had attended several business meetings of the Christian Democrat Party, who, although mostly Catholics, were anxious to incorporate the Protestants. He said that he thought that whatever happened, the Christian Democrats would be effectively dominated by Catholics. He said that it had struck him when reading the Christian Democrat Programme that it was almost exactly the same as that of the Communists in Cologne. Both parties promised many things which could not be achieved except at the wish of the Occupying Powers, such as the reconstruction of the German towns and industry, and the nationalization of public utilities and of many industries.

Bender thought that the leaders of the Christian Democrat Party were amiable men but that they were old, out of touch, unrealistic, ineffective. At a foundation meeting of the party he had noticed that the younger section of the audience, some poor priests and monks, were dissatisfied and that they took a more realistic and forward-looking attitude than that of the party leaders.

He thought that the Civilian Administration of Cologne (the German part of it) was pretty corrupt. The members of the Civil Government lived as comfortably as possible and tried to install themselves in public institutions run by the churches and hospitals so that their families would be well looked after, and their wives would not have to queue for rations. He had heard a member of the Civil Government say to his employer: "Why, your wife doesn't have to queue for food, does she?" Bender disapproved very much of these people and he thought that they were too out of touch with the ordinary life of Cologne to be able to understand the problems of their fellow citizens.

This is a difficult problem. It is obvious that to some extent the German administrators of Germany must be favoured by the Occupiers, but the very fact that they are so favoured marks them with a taint of collaboration in the eyes of many Germans, and also prevents many idealistic Germans from collaborating with us.

The conversation turned to culture and Bender said how much he admired the work of Professor Kroll in getting concerts going. But he added: "All the same, that isn't culture. The Nazis knew very well that if they called the cinema and music culture then they could produce good films and good concerts and go on pretending that Germany was a cultured country. Now everyone continues to think that films and music are culture. But really culture begins with the knowledge of science and art when they give men a taste for the free development of their ideas, and a critical spirit. Music soothes. It creates a complete self-contained inner world which has no quarrel with the outer world. Even when it tries to be revolutionary, as with Beethoven, its application to external conditions outside music is so unprecise that it only communicates a vague revolutionary enthusiasm to any cause to which it is attached. The Nazis realized this very well and they simply appropriated the two *dream arts,* music and the cinema, stuck them on to visions of the Hitler Revolution, and called them culture.

We went on talking about culture. Bender went on to say that one of the most wrong and prevalent ideas in Germany was that culture was a kind of huge drinking cup to be passed round the whole German people, from which everyone could take a little sip. "Culture is not for the masses," he said, "but only for the happy few. And in Germany this is even more true than in any other country. For German culture has no deep roots in the life of the whole people, as have French, Italian and Spanish culture. German culture began abruptly in the eighteenth century. Moreover, German philosophy preceded and greatly influenced the literature of Goethe, Schiller, Hoelderlin, and so on. Therefore there is something abstract and theoretical about the best German writing which makes it less generally acceptable to the masses than any other literature in the world. Educated French people can understand *Les Caractères* of La Bruyère and imbibe wisdom from it. But how very few Germans can understand even *Faust*."

8. Wuppertal

MY CAR CONTINUED TO BE OUT OF ORDER. EVERY MORNING at breakfast, and again in the evening, my driver reported lack of progress to me. After a few days, I thought it would be well for me to go along myself and speak to the Quartermaster Sergeant at the Repair Shop. So one morning I walked along to the garage outside Bonn with my driver.

I talked quite a lot to him on our walk. I was worried about his having nothing to do. He said that he was also getting "browned off" as all he could do now was go every day to the garage and watch them working at the car. He said that they had tested every part of it and replaced every part that seemed at all weak. In fact it was practically a new engine, but still it would not go. Theoretically the car ought to be in perfect condition but in fact it behaved exactly as it had done a week ago. He said he thought the trouble must be the carburettor—the one part they had not been able to replace.

He cheered up a bit telling me that he had quite a lot of fun in the evenings as now he had a nice girl, aged eighteen.

I felt that it was perhaps my duty to say something so I asked him whether he "took precautions to avoid getting the girl into trouble?" He looked most astonished and then he flushed and said: "I never touch her. I wouldn't think of doing so. That wouldn't be any pleasure for her nor for me, sir." I was somewhat taken aback by this reply. He told me that he thought it would be very wrong, especially in times like these, to leave a girl with a baby. I agreed about this. He said: "It makes me very angry sometimes, sir, when I read the newspapers, to see what they think our fellows do when they fraternize out here. As a matter of fact, very few of them do what they think at all. I myself wouldn't dream of it. Yet even my girl at home thinks the same thing."

He told me that one night he and another chap had gone to the fair in Bonn with two girls and that on their way back, when they were seeing their girls home, they ran into some Germans who were attacking some other German girls who had been fraternizing with our men. So they had a free fight with the Germans, rescued the girls and escorted them home as well.

At the garage the engineers were already working on the car which was considered the most "serious case" they had. It had a reputation rather similar to that which Rudi Bach once had at the hospital in Bonn. They told me that they had tested some parts of it nine times, and that they had gone sixty miles yesterday in search of a carburettor. I stayed, and they explained to me all the details of what they had done. They were now for the third time experimenting with the pump. When this was finished we gave the Humber a trial run again. It ran, but it back-fired all the time, and blue flames shot out of the carburettor.

The QM Sergeant also talked to me about the car, with almost as much concern as the doctors had talked at the hospital about Rudi Bach. He said he thought "she would pull through" and that I could rely on them to do their utmost, as they did not like to be defeated by any problem.

In the afternoon I went with my driver to see a Transport Officer, as I had got to the stage when I needed a witness that my car was broken down, in order to get another one. This Transport Officer was a young man with a very white face and deepset eyes. I left my driver in a waiting-room while I talked with the officer. He was sympathetic and asked many questions about the Humber. I said: "My driver is in the next room, perhaps you would like to speak with him?" Quite a new expression came on the Transport Officer's face, and he said "yes," tersely.

The driver came in and the officer addressed him abruptly: "Are you this officer's driver?" "Yes, sir." "Well, has the car broken down?" "Yes, sir." "Well, if we're going to do anything about it, for a start it might be helpful if you stood to attention in my office." "Yes, sir."

The officer got very little information out of my driver who suddenly seemed quite stupid, and who, while standing all the while at attention, nevertheless kept looking sideways past me out of the window, and blowing slightly out of the corner of his mouth, with a longing expression in his eyes as though he wanted to fly out of the window.

Finally the officer rang up a Colonel to whom he spoke in quite a new voice, different from the one he used with me, and different from that he used with the driver. He suggested to the Colonel that he should ring up the garage and ask them to get a move on.

When we left the office, my driver exploded: "A Guards' Officer! A Guards' Officer! The bloody Guards! If you hadn't been there, I'd have told him what I thought of him, sir." I said that I was glad he had said nothing, as it would have been awkward for me to have to take sides against him. "It isn't that," he said. "It is that if I'd been alone with him, there wouldn't have been a witness. I could have said exactly what I liked and he'd never have been able to prove it. The Guards' Officers!"

The next morning I went in a town car with a German driver to Wuppertal, by way of Cologne and through some villages and small towns quite unaffected by the war. Here was charming architecture, half-timbered houses which look much neater than our Elizabethan houses, and houses with walls covered with blue slates rounded like fish-scales. Wuppertal is an industrial town in a very narrow valley. It consists really of several towns which have all grown together into a large town along the river Wupper. There is a remarkable overhanging tram line which runs above the Wupper, being supported by straddling iron trestles with feet on either bank. The tram hangs suspended downwards from this line with its wheels on the roof and the bottom of the tram hanging downwards. Most of this system of girders had escaped damage.

In Wuppertal, I went through my usual library routine. I called on the Commanding Officer, a French Canadian, who sent me at once to see the Mayor. The Mayor said that the chief librarian was a Dr. Van der Biele who had been turned down by the Military Government because he had organized a distribution of War Books during the war. The Mayor, however, was in favour of Van der Biele and said that he had no choice but to distribute War Books. This Mayor did not have the crushed defeated appearance of most of the Mayors I had met. He was a grey-haired energetic business man with an elastic stride.

I told the Mayor that Military Government must decide and that if they maintained their attitude to Van der Biele some one else must be found. The Mayor then sent me to see Stadtrat Dr. Bragard who took me along to the *Stadtbibliothek* where I met Dr. Springmann, Van der Biele's Deputy.

Later, I discovered that Captain Heslop, Education Officer, had the library situation well in hand and that my visit was unnecessary. All over the Ruhr, I found that on the cultural side there were Education Officers full of energy and good ideas who were doing their utmost to open libraries, produce newspapers, encourage concerts and other performances.

Dr. Springmann looked sad and old and gentle and I liked him. The library was a large square granite and concrete building of the style of about 1907. Stadtrat Dr. Bragard was a white-faced tight-lipped little authoritarian who started ordering Dr. Springmann about as soon as we arrived. The telephone bell rang in the next room and Dr. Springmann left the room to answer it. Two minutes later, Dr. Bragard thrust his furious little head through the door and shouted: "Dr. Springmann! Dr. Springmann! Why are you keeping the officer waiting?" When Dr. Springmann had appeared, Dr. Bragard said to me: "Of course, Dr. Springmann has not the qualifications of *Wissenschaft* which one would expect from a librarian of Wuppertal."

After this, I drove to the Officers' Mess outside Wuppertal, in pleasant country, for lunch. It consisted mostly of Civilian Military Government Officers. One of them took me up to his room to wash. Some officers were there looking at photographs. One of these appeared to me to be a sack filled with mud, and while I was washing I wondered idly what it was. It vaguely resembled a human form. Later I gathered from the remarks of the officers among themselves that a mass grave of Russians, Poles and French had been discovered in the woods about five miles from the Mess. There were several more photographs, some of separate bodies, and some of heaps of them.

After this we went in to lunch. The officers started complaining rather bitterly because some of them were having their cars taken away from them, to be given (it seemed) to German business men. "Believe me," someone said, "the Germans must take us for mugs. Sometimes I wonder whether it's we who've conquered them or they who've conquered us. A lot of them must be thinking that they still have the better of these English mugs."

Everyone seemed to connect the fact that their cars had been taken away with the discovery of the mass grave, though it was difficult to see the connection.

There were also one or two remarks to the effect that after what they had seen they were sick to see English business **men kowtowing** to German business men.

In one or two of the photographs the Mayor, with whom I had spoken this morning, and other Germans prominent in Wuppertal were photographed with the bodies, so that when the photographs were published the readers recognizing their own Mayor and other functionaries, would see that they were authentic. It was extraordinary to contrast the blank, expressionless, reluctant look on the Mayor's face in the photograph, with his brisk, business-like appearance when I had seen him. In the photograph he himself and his colleagues looked almost dead. The officers told me that the Mayor, when they had discovered the grave, first of all said that he knew nothing about it. Later, on being interrogated, he said that he did recall it but that it was "quite in order": the bodies were of "criminal elements" who had been shot for sound reasons. However, the grave was not marked or notified in any way. Another grave in the neighbourhood, known to contain eighty-eight bodies, has not yet been discovered.

On my way home, I noticed an extraordinary sight. Every one of the large houses on the hillside above Wuppertal has been destroyed. They are scattered over a wide area and are many hundreds of yards apart from each other.

Just as I arrived in the centre of Bonn, another car stopped very suddenly in front of my car and an officer with a white, podgy face jumped out. He rushed up to my driver but when he saw me he hesitated and said: "Oh, I was just going to give your driver a rocket for dangerous driving. But I thought it was only the Boche I had to deal with. I didn't realize there was an English officer with him." I said nothing and we drove on. The only danger had been from this officer stopping suddenly in front of us.

A German told me that Wuppertal had had two of the worst raids in the war. It had not been raided at all and then in two raids it was wiped out. The people did not know how to behave during raids and in the first raid liquid phosphorus was used for the first time on Germany. People rushed through the streets like torches, with liquid phosphorus in flame covering them. Some of them jumped into the river Wupper in an effort to put the flames out, and they were drowned. He added that an extraordinary feature of this raid was that single aircraft had destroyed all the large houses on the hillside above the valley, one by one in separate attacks.

Europe is full of these horrible hidden graves left by the Germans, and discovered by search or by accident. An officer told me of a similar discovery when Holland was liberated in March 1945. He had a friend, a young doctor, who was clever and tolerant. He was therefore surprised to learn that this young man had personally arranged that his young sister, aged seventeen, should have her hair shaved off because she had gone out one night in a motor car with a German officer. He asked his friend to explain how he could have done this. A few days later the Dutch doctor asked him to go to a police station to meet one of the foremost criminologists of Holland. At the police station, the criminologist, an elderly man with a long white beard, was questioning a Dutch collaborator. The collaborator, to save his life, said that he would show them some things which would interest them. He took them to a place among sand dunes, and he said: "Dig here." There was no sign of anything but they started digging and two or three feet under the sand they found a body. Altogether in the course of the next few days, the police dug up seventy-five bodies. The criminologist pointed out that most of these bodies were not of people who had been killed before being buried. They had simply had their legs broken or they had been hit over the head and then buried while they were still alive. They were mostly doctors, teachers, journalists, writers, who had been held in custody of the Nazis who, losing their heads during the last days of the Occupation, had disposed of thousands of prisoners in this way.

9. Goebbels

THE CAR REMAINED IN A VERY BAD STATE. HOWEVER, ONE day we managed to get it to go to Aachen and almost all the way back before we got stuck a few miles outside Bonn, from where we had to be towed.

In Aachen I did all the usual things in the usual order. I

discovered that the chief librarian is a prisoner of war, but there is a Fräulein Wurz who is taking the library over. As they had thrown away a good many Nazi books in Aachen, I took away with me copies of some of Goebbels's works, some novels by Ernst Jünger and Otto Dietrich's *Mit Hitler in die Macht*. I have spent some time now in reading these books.

Goebbels is a magnetic writer for young people. He communicates the excitement of the Nazi movement luridly but effectively. One can feel thrilled even to-day by passages from his diary such as that in which he describes the sensations of the Nazi leaders in 1933 when they came to power:

30 January 1933. It is all like a dream. The Wilhelmstrasse belongs to us. Already the Führer is working in the *Reichskanzlei*. We are standing upstairs at the window, while hundreds of thousands on hundreds of thousands of people march in the flickering light of torches past the grey Reichspräsident and the young Chancellor and shout their joy and thanksgiving to them.

At midday we all sat in the Kaiserhof and waited. The Führer was with the Reichspräsident. An indescribable sense of excitement made us all hold our breath. Outside, between the Kaiserhof and the Chancellory people stood and waited and were silent. What was going on within?

Our hearts were torn between doubt, hope, happiness and discouragement. We had been disappointed too often to be able to believe without any restraint in the great miracle.

Ceaselessly we looked from a window out on to the door of the Chancellory. This is where the Führer had to come out. One would be able to tell from the expression on his face how things had gone.

Painful hours of waiting. At last a car turned round the corner of the entrance. The masses called out and shouted greetings. They seemed to guess that the great turning point had been reached or had already been passed.

The Führer comes!

A few minutes later he is with us in the room. He says nothing, none of us say anything. But his eyes are full of tears. So it had come to this!

The Führer has been called upon to be chancellor. He has already put his oath into the hands of the President. The hour of decision has arrived. Germany stands at its historic turning point.

We all are dumb with emotion. Each of us shakes the Führer's hand, and it is as though our troth to each other were pledged again and renewed.

Wonderful, how simple the Führer is in his greatness, how great in his simplicity.

One opens a book and reads a page like this in a public library in Germany, or in one of the towns of the Ruhr, one turns up an old illustrated paper and sees photographs of a swaying mass of people cheering the local Nazi leader (without there being a discernible trait of doubt on a single face of all those faces) with somewhat the same emotion as one stumbles on a mass grave. It is, indeed, the same phenomenon of mass hysteria on the greatest possible scale. Even the ruins of the German Chancellory in Berlin convey an emotion not entirely unlike that which the Chancellory conveyed on its days of greatest jubilation. The day of triumph is here identical with the day of downfall, the day of shamelessness with the day of shame and disgrace.

In all Nazi literature there is a paradox which has puzzled many observers but which is really one of the keys to the character of the whole movement. This is the combination of most extreme disingenuousness with most extreme frankness. It strikes one again and again that the Nazis tell the most elaborate lies only to expose them themselves with the utmost pride. The most illuminating example of this paradoxical behaviour is Hitler's famous remark that in deceiving the people it is necessary to tell the biggest lie possible, because the greater the lie the more avid they are to believe it. At first, it seems amazing that he should expose his own method so flagrantly, until on reflection one sees that it is itself an example of the method he recommends. If people will believe any lie, however large, they will also not believe any truth, however evident, if they do not wish to do so. And Hitler realized that nothing flattered his "masses" so much as talk about the "masses": for sometimes they liked to think of themselves as the great, great-hearted masses, and sometimes they liked as it were to be treated confidentially and separately, and to take the side of Hitler in despising the "masses." For no one thinks of himself, except when it flatters him to do so, as "the masses." Thus Hitler and Goebbels played a double game with their followers.

But above all the game was one of creating and sustaining hysterical tensions. Thus even in this entry of Goebbels's *Journal* for 30th January 1933, on the day of his greatest triumph, there is a sense of implicit disaster. "Anything might happen," "it is all a dream," "our hearts are torn," Goebbels says, and the opposites of calamity and triumph are played on the whole time. There is a sense of risk, of breathlessness in the Nazi's most confident moments.

Of course, no amount of propagandist ingenuity would succeed, if there were not also a genuine faith which integrates the violent and disparate opposites of the Nazi methods. What is genuine here is a real belief in extremism for its own sake, faith in their own destiny, whether it led to triumph or to disaster, and a camaraderie which enabled the Nazis to feel that all their actions were purified in the blood of their martyrs and in the purgative strength of their emotions.

The general guilt of Germany is an open secret in the published writings and speeches of Hitler and Goebbels. Guilt lies in being captivated by the speeches of the serpent and in being without the sense of values which can resist temptation. The diaries of Goebbels and his history *Kampf um Berlin* could only appeal, one would think, to readers of sensational detective fiction and of children's fairy stories. Yet, even though the work of other Nazi writers was unread, Goebbels and Hitler most certainly were read.

The detective-story element in Goebbels's *Kampf um Berlin* is the perpetual hunt of a ruthless scientifically-minded Nazi sleuth for the Communist or the Jewish criminal who must be hounded out and destroyed, even though the police (under Jewish police leaders, such as Bernard Weiss, Vice-Police President of Berlin) are on the side of the criminal and working against the Nazi detective who has taken the law in his own hands. As in detective stories, the detective himself does not set up to be a saint. He uses the methods of his opponents; above all he is "scientific" and has lots of theories, though, at the same time, with characteristic lack of logic, he has a healthy contempt for mere theoreticians and regards himself as a practical man achieving practical results.

There is a Nazi illustrator called Mjoelnir whose work repays study. His illustrations of the Nazis fighting Communists and Jews are exactly those suited to a boys' adventure book or to the books of the German writer Karl May. They are below the level of Sherlock Holmes. Goebbels wholeheartedly admires Mjoelnir, whom he regards as a master of a *"Gott-begnadetes Künstlertum."*

The fairy-tale side of the Nazi myth goes deeper than the *Boys' Own Paper* and amateur detective side. In this, Hitler is the Fairy Prince whose character and actions are perfect. Communists and Jews are the wicked spirits, the subhuman forces who do not have to be regarded as human. In fact, to accept their claim to be regarded as human is to be seduced by them. Here again, though, as in fairy stories, there is plenty of room for all-devouring cruelty and no bones are made about this in Nazi literature.

Another element of this writing is baseness, vulgarity, *Gemeinheit*. The grossest of Nazi vulgarities is their repulsive confidence trick of taking the reader into their secrets, especially when they are talking about "propaganda," a term which is universally accepted (not only by the Nazis) as a kind of honourable dishonourableness. Goebbels writes: "Propaganda has only one goal; and in politics this goal is only one thing: the winning of the masses. Every means which serves this goal is good. And every means which eludes this goal is bad."

After this, and parallel passages in *Mein Kampf*, it is very difficult to say that the Nazi followers were deceived by the Nazi leaders. Goebbels and Hitler did not leave a single one of their followers with this excuse. They went so far out of their way not to do so, that perhaps it is not fanciful to feel that at moments these guilty souls were actuated by a real desire to implicate those who followed them in their own damnation and to impose on them their own guilt. Nazi propaganda was a conscious and deliberate deception, practised by people who said "we are now going to deceive ourselves," people who saw the label "poison" on the bottle. Anyone who "took" Nazi propaganda must have been as conscious of drugging himself as anyone who takes opium.

The most appalling and also the most enthralling thing about Goebbels's writing is its note of an impersonal confidence which certainly does not come quite from Goebbels himself. It comes, rather, from a feeling that he is supplying the evil which hundreds and thousands of Germans want.

The power of this evil is that it goes back to a very deep source and is completely genuine. All Goebbels's later works are so tainted with propaganda and have such an official aspect that it is difficult to calculate what is genuine and what is the "party line." One has to go back to Goebbels's first work, a novel called *Michael*, published in 1929, to discover that the real Goebbels is essentially the Nazi Goebbels, from the days when he was a rebellious student at Heidelberg to his dramatic death in the Reichschancellory in 1945.

Michael is a novel written in the form of a day-by-day journal. It is an extremely subjective book and the characterization scarcely extends beyond that of the chaotic young hero who is in revolt against everything and everyone, and in search only of some phenomenon in the world as turbulent and undisciplined as himself. As a novel, *Michael* does not exist, and even within its own limits as an expressionist document, it scarcely rises above schoolgirlish journalism. There are passages which are poetic on this level of writing:

> *Am offenen Fenster:*
> *Ein letztes Hauchen*
> *Von müdem Vogelsang*
> *Und duftendem Flieder*
> *Trägt mir der Abendwind*
> *Ins Zimmer.*
> *Ich kann nicht schlafen!*
>
> (At the open window
> The wind carries
> A last breath
> Of tired bird-song
> And scented lilac
> Into my room.
> I cannot sleep!)

Very little happens in *Michael*. The hero is a young student, his mind full of memories of 1918, who is supposed to be studying at Heidelberg (actually he never studies anything). He has love affairs and friendships. His relationship with people on whom he fastens his attention has two aspects. One is that others should believe in his "demon," his genius. The other is that they are his opponents. These two passionate impulses, together with his passionate nationalism, and a perpetual restless desire to transcend the narrow boundaries of his existence in post-war Germany on the wave of some tremendous emotion, leave him no room to be interested in human beings as human beings, and no room for self-criticism. Occasionally he has a sense of failure and of despair, as he passes from one emotional crisis to another. Yet he has a great faith in himself, and if one asks how such a person can have such faith, the answer is that the experience of constant turmoil gives him a convincing sense of the reality of his own existence, and it is this which he above all demands from life: to suffer, to be mad, to experience a sense of ecstasy.

It is difficult to imagine that anyone can have thought *Michael* to be other than a book by a criminal written for criminals, and I do not really believe that anyone with the least enlightenment ever did think so. It is the type of Nazi book, like *Mein Kampf* itself, which benefited greatly from a dilemma of our culture and our literary criticism. Every serious critic who judged it on literary grounds considered it of no importance. To protect ourselves from books such as *Mein Kampf*, *Michael*, and a great deal of crime and gangster fiction, we need a new branch of criticism, which considers certain books as social phenomena. Very few critics (George Orwell in England is one of the very few) have attempted this kind of criticism.

The story of *Michael* is slight. Michael becomes a worker in a mine and he is killed by a fall of coal, but not before he has discovered the Nazi truth in the beer cellars of Munich. It is the observations, the prophecies and intuitions of *Michael* which do have a certain genius.

What is genuine about this novel? It is full of crude propaganda and of ideas which it is difficult to take any more seriously than Friedrich Gundolf, the famous Heidelberg professor, was disposed to take the young Goebbels's atrocious verse drama on the subject of Jesus, the writing of which is described in *Michael*. Many people would say that the sense of defeat, of reaction against post-war decadence, of national humiliation, was what is most genuine in *Michael*. But there is something less dramatic and perhaps profounder than this, which is simply the sense of boredom with modern civilization. It is difficult to say that the material conditions described in this novel are such as to justify the chaotic violence of the feelings expressed; feelings which were those of many thousands of young Germans. But frustrated nationalism joins forces here with a sense of *ennui* which is to be found in Baudelaire, Carlyle, Wagner and many other European artists. Michael is in revolt against socialism as much as against capitalism. He cannot be said to have any great love of his fellow Germans, or, indeed, of anyone but himself. He is conscious of a sense of isolation which is not characteristic of earlier nationalists and patriots. If German nationalism still has a great appeal for him, this is because it produced the last war which corresponds to the chaos of his own soul, and he feels that it is the one force in the world capable of producing a great chaos again, perhaps even a final condition of chaos or else a condition of German triumph in which the ecstatic warriors who live in order to transcend their own limitations in orgies of self-assertion, will trample on the world.

The message of *Michael* is "Evil, be thou my good," but there is also an attempt to prove that evil is good because the

German evil is made virtuous by destroying other evils. Motherlove and love of children are invoked to gild the pill of undiluted evil. But Michael's reason for being sentimental about children is curious: it is that children are "like nature," that is to say, "heartless and cruel." Perhaps his hidden reason for devotion to his mother, is that love of one's mother excuses one from having to love anyone else:

> Mother!
> One needs to have nothing else, except a mother.
> A mother who is not everything to her children—friend, teacher, confidant, source of joy and firm pride, spur, brake, accuser, reconciler, judge and pardoner—has clearly failed in her calling to be a mother.

One can discover in *Michael* all the Nazi and Fascist symptoms.

A belief strongly held by the Fascist leaders is that statesmen are frustrated poets and artists who become acknowledged legislators of the world. Thus Goebbels writes:

> The true poet is a kind of amateur photographer of life. For a poem is nothing else but a snapshot taken by the lens of the artistic soul. Art is the expression of feeling. The artist is distinguished from him who is not an artist by the fact that he can express that which he feels. . . . The statesman is also an artist. For him the people are that which a stone is for the sculptor. Leader and masses, that is exactly the same problem as painter and colour.

In his rôle of artist, the statesman is an expressionist:

> To-day we are all expressionists. Men who want to make the world outside themselves take the form of their life within themselves.
> The expressionist builds within himself a new world. His secret and his power are the forces within his own passionate nature. The world of his inner thought breaks to pieces on reality.

The expressionist world-feeling is explosive. It is an autocratic sensation of its own being.

Michael explains and defends all his own actions by saying that he is following his "demon" (his genius):

I think and act as I must think and act. That is what everyone does who does not belong to the herd. A demon operates in us, who leads us along a pre-ordained path. One can do nothing against this demon.

When Michael says this, his girl friend protests:

"In politics you think like an artist. That is dangerous for your own life and your career."

"What is my career? I still have two strong arms with which I can work."

He leaves this girl because she does not believe sufficiently in his "demon."

God, for Michael, is Will—his own Will.

God is Will, and the Will loves God.

My God is a God of the Strong. He does not care for the smell of incense and the dishonourable flattery of the multitude.

I stand free and proud in front of him with uplifted head, as he made me, and I recognize myself joyfully and freely in front of him.

The true German remains all his life a seeker after God.

Michael identifies himself with Christ, though he thinks that he can improve on Him. For he cannot quite forgive Christ for having been crucified. Christ is the great enemy of the Jews, whom he drove out of the Temple with whips. There is the difficulty that Christ himself was a Jew, but Michael's passionate intuition easily overcomes this: "Christ cannot have been a Jew. I do not have to demonstrate this scientifically. It is a fact." Christ is hard and embittered, and the implication is that if He were living to-day He would be the greatest enemy of the Jews.

Goebbels

He would be a German nationalist; He would declare war against money, and also against Karl Marx.

The Jew according to Goebbels's brand of German Christianity (which he also calls Christian Socialism) is the incarnation of evil:

> For me the Jew is simply a physical malady. I become sick and faint with disgust at the mere sight of him.
> The Jew's whole existence is directed against us. I cannot hate him, I can only despise him. He has disgraced our people, soiled our ideal, undermined the strength of our nation, fouled our morality and corrupted our manners.
> He is the abscess on the body of our sick people.
> Religion? How naive you are. What has this got to do with religion or with Christianity? Either he throws us to the ground, or we make him harmless. No other way out is possible.
> Peace? Can the lungs make peace with the tuberculous bacilli? . . .
> No one can love God who is not also capable of hating the devil. Whoever loves his own people must hate the destroyer of his own people, must hate him from the depths of his soul.

The society which Michael is perpetually seeking is only to be found in war. War is his relationship with other human beings which is most natural to him. It puts him in the right passional relationship of hate and love with his fellow beings, at the same time it satisfies his craving to experience the sense of his own existence at the greatest possible pitch of intensity. It provides him with an excuse for not having to do other kinds of work, and in war he is both able to play the part of the devil and feel at the same time that he is fighting against a devil—his opponent, and behind the face of his opponent the hidden form of the eternal Jew. War is also man's means of compensating himself for the fact that he does not experience that sense of existence which is the privilege of woman—bearing children.

Hertha Holk, Michael's first girl friend (the one who does not sufficiently appreciate his "demon") says, with characteristic lack of sensibility:

"War is terrible."
"That is a fact of no significance," replies Michael. "No reasonable human being has ever denied that war is terrible. But at the same time to wish to do away with war would be exactly like wishing to do without women bringing children into the world. That also is terrible. Everything living is terrible.

"All one can do against war is to take measures protecting oneself: a people must arm itself so that other peoples lose the desire to take away its rights."

Even Hertha Holk is overwhelmed by Michael's demon at this point. "In you there dwell a poet and a soldier," she exclaims. "Are you also a musician?" "A bit of one," is the answer.

Occasionally Michael has visions. They are all of an ecstatic, violent nature. Here is one of them:

I put on my helmet, I draw my dagger and I declaim
The Crown of Lilies (Lilencron).
Sometimes this mood overcomes me.
To be a soldier! To stand at one's post!
A soldier in the service of the Revolution of his people.

Then I think with horror of fire and destruction.

I see houses being destroyed and villages smoulder in the evening light. Pillars of fire ascend. Noise and thunder of firearms.

I see vomiting eyes and hear the groans of dying men. My hands are black with gunpowder, my coat is red with blood. No, war is not beautiful.

I hear loud words of command, cries of Hurrah. I shout also: Hurrah! Hurrah!

I am no longer a man. A savage fury overcomes me. I sweat blood.

I shout "Forwards! Forwards! I want to be a hero."

I tear out my heart. What does a heart matter? I throw it into the storm of fire.
I am a hero, a God, a Saviour!
I myself bleed. My arms hang down powerless.
I have been hit.
I become tired. I sink down.
I lose my consciousness.

What kind of a God is this, one is left wondering. That Michael feels affinities with Satan is evident. There are desires to be "a flame," "Pan" as well as Jesus Christ.

Work in the mine also gives him the feeling of demoniac possession, the pursuit of which is Michael's sole aim in life, not just for himself but for the whole of society. Here is the first experience in the mine:

To work again. I do not stop. This work possesses me like a demon.
I strike blow on blow. I strike on my own hands. Intolerable pain!
The blood runs on the thumbs and fingers. I hold them in my mouth where they burn like fire.
Strike! Strike! The work spurs me on. I am its servant, its slave, its dog.
I shall be incapable of stopping until I fall to the ground.
I cry out, I howl like a hungry animal.
Fire leaps from the stone. I strike flame! I strike light!
I am no longer a man. I am a Titan! A God!

Intellectual effort fills Michael with sense of emptiness and despair, which he endeavours to escape from in demoniacally possessed action:

A sense of hopelessness overwhelms me like an elemental power.
I hate this soft Heidelberg!
Restlessness! Yearning!

I long for work.
I can endure no longer this life amongst dead books.
I must shape something. More than intellect works in us.
We must create a new conception of work.
Intellect is lifeless. It cannot provide us with the sense of existence.
How can anyone write books and collect knowledge when the Reich lies in ruins?

The idea of the Jews is a fantasy in Michael's mind, a bully's rationalization of his own cowardly contempt for the weak. His attitude to the Russians is quite different, and to-day it seems prophetic. He sees himself reflected in the achievement of Lenin, and also in the nihilism of *The Possessed* by Dostoievsky. He admires and yet he hates Russia. And, of course, he is fascinated. Anyone reading *Michael* would say that Russia was for the hero the abyss into which it was impossible for him not to throw himself.

On the boundaries of the great problem of Europe lies the old, the new Russia. Russia is the Past, perhaps also the Future, but in no way the Present. For the Russian Present is only soap-bubbles beneath which lies the acrid alkali. In the Russian soil there broods the solution of a great puzzle. The spirit of Dostoievsky flies pregnant with futurity over the silent, dreaming land. If Russia awakens, then the world will behold a great national miracle.

A national miracle? Yes, exactly so. Political miracles only happen to nations. The International is only an exercise of the understanding, directed against the blood. The miracle of a people never lies in the brain, always in the blood.

What is called in Russia the International is a mish-mash invented by Jewish lawyers and only existing within the political arena on account of the overwhelming will of one man: Lenin.

Without Lenin, no Bolshevism.

Once again. Men make history. Bad men also.

In Russia the peasants have been freed. Have they? Yes, to the extent that it was impossible to do otherwise. And there is no Marxism even there any more.

"Property is theft," say the upright class-fighters. Lenin gave every Russian peasant land as his property. Since then a hundred million thieves live in Russia.

Dostoievsky is the incarnation of the demon of the devil which Goebbels himself would like to be:

> He writes down that which he beholds, what his demon the devil in his brain and in his soul reveals to him in letters of fire. He writes because writing is still in the nineteenth century one of the possible modes of existence. The political solution was yet unborn. He writes because his love of Russia, his hatred of the foreigner, of the West, burn in his soul. One has to accept him as unique. He comes from nowhere. And at the same time he always remains Russian.

Here is the acknowledgement that Nazism is not just a postwar symptom. It has roots in the nineteenth century, and one can sum up the impulse behind it as the desire of the individual to become a self-consuming and perhaps a world-consuming flame in the modern world. There is little doubt that Goebbels, if he had read more, would have recognized himself in the demoniac aspect of Byron, and in the Satanism of Baudelaire.

However, whereas Baudelaire knew that Satan was Satan, but preferred Satan to respectability, the Nazis called Satan, Christ. In justice to the Nazis it may be said, though, that perhaps it requires more courage to put Satanic philosophy into action than to make it a literary fashion, and that perhaps, in order to put it into action, it had to pretend to be Christian.

The large prophetic issue in *Michael* is the conflict between the German soul and the Russian soul, between panSlavism and pan-Germanism. The "West" in the German sense means simply the coalition of all the demoniac and orgiastic forces of the West on the German side against the East.

Our entire German history is nothing else but the continual chain of the struggle of the German soul against its opponents.

The German soul resembles Faust (is Faustian). In it there is the driving force of toil with a realization of all its opportunities, and the eternal search to free itself from the spirit.

There is a German ideology, just as there is a Russian one. One day in the future the two ideas will be measured one against the other.

There is a shadowy character in the novel called Ivan Wienurowsky against whom Michael symbolically measures himself. At first he is rather fascinated by this Russian. But later he becomes aware of him as an opponent, *the* opponent, indeed:

Russia is a danger for us which we have to overcome. But in order to overcome it we must understand it.

At last I am reaching the point when I understand the inner being of Ivan Wienurowsky.

He is a very unhappy man. Pan-Slavism has ground him to the earth.

I have not yet compelled Ivan Wienurowsky to submit to my domination.

One of Michael's most powerful visions concerns Ivan Wienurowsky. It is a vision in which the devil in Ivan is completely identified with the devil in Michael—his vision takes place after Michael has had the accident in the mine:

I seek green. I find nothing.
A tree, a bush, a flower.
Nothing. Everything is grey. Short as though shaved away.
Only the towers, the chimneys, the masts, the factories, reach upwards.
I go farther, stagger farther.
Quicker, ever quicker.

I begin to run; I sprint, I chase. I fly like the wind. I rush through the streets, into the city and out again.
Out! Out! Into the fields.
But everywhere, towers, chimneys, masts, factories!
Grey upon grey and sunshine above.
White sunshine.
Am I then mad? I dream?
Has the world gone under?
Do no human beings live any more? Only beasts still, black beasts? Devils, devils in mines?
Am I myself a beast, a black beast, a devil, a devil of the mines?
I am as though whipped on by demons.
One of them sits inside me, observing me, another, a second one also.
Inexorable. Sharp. Critical.
Ivan Wienurowsky!
Now I have you, damnable dog!
You beast! You devil! You Satan!
Come here, I'll cast you out. I'll cast you out by your throat.
You will never down me. Never! Never!
We shall see who is the stronger.
I laugh. I cry.
People came up to me, people who look questioningly at me, who laugh, talk, point at me.
I run farther.
Farther! Farther!
To the end of the earth!
I fight with Ivan Wienurowsky! He is nimble as a cat.
But I am stronger than he.
Now I have him by the throat.
I thrust him to the ground.
He lies there!
With the death rattle, with blood running from his eyes.
Die, you carrion!
I tread upon his skull.
And now I am free!
The last opponent thrust to the earth.
The poison is out.

I am free!
I remain! I remain!
I will free myself. Free myself with my own strength.
1 will show a way, strike a breach, be an example.
I throw myself on the ground and kiss the earth.
Hard brown earth.
German earth!
I come home late at night and fling myself as though dead across my bed.

In spite of this fantasy, by an extraordinary and penetrating intuition, the truth of which Goebbels was doubtless unconscious of, Michael dies shortly after making this entry in his Journal, calling out as his last words, "Ivan, you fiend."

Michael cannot be called literature. It has intuitive qualities of a greatly inferior quality to those which are found in some of the books of D. H. Lawrence. Yet it is a document of a certain interest. As literature it even has a certain indirect interest, for it confirms the intuitions of poets. A Macbeth who spoke for himself, without having the aid of genius of Shakespeare would express just such thoughts as: "Now I am free! The poison is out!" In fact, the thoughts of Goebbels with regard to Russia, are identical with those of Macbeth with regard to Banquo and his sons. As long as Russia exists, he must feel:

> Then comes my fit again: I had else been perfect;
> Whole as the marble, founded as the rock;
> As broad and general as the casing air:
> But now I am cabin'd, cribb'd, confined bound in
> To saucy doubts and fears.

If a book such as *Michael* had been published as a document written by an ordinary murderer after he had committed a crime and been hanged, it would excite considerable excitement among criminologists and the general public. Yet this book, written by one of the greatest murderers of all history—Goebbels—four years before the Nazis came to power, has never been discussed outside Germany. The copy in my possession is the ninth edition of forty-one thousand copies. Unlike most books by the Nazis, it continued to be read, as the ticket at the end of the volume shows. It was taken out of Aachen Library on an average of once every two months between 1940 and 1943.

10. Newspapers

ON 20TH SEPTEMBER THE HUMBER HAD A SLIGHT ATTACK OF recovery. I made an attempt to get it to Duesseldorf. After going very fast for four miles, it stopped in a rainstorm on the autobahn between Bonn and Cologne. My driver decided that the pump was wrong and he got out to repair it. After he had taken it to pieces and put it back, no petrol came through the pipe leading to it from the tank at the back of the car. He undid the cap of the petrol tank and blew down the hole. There was some pressure of air in the tank and petrol squirted back at him into his eyes, mouth and nose. He was practically blinded for five or ten minutes. Three little German boys who were present at this scene were in ecstasies of hysterical joy. They rolled over on the ground roaring with laughter, and, for the next hour, while we waited dismally in the car, they imitated to each other the expression on his face when he fell back into the road. This was one of those moments when our Occupation suddenly appeared like all Occupations: one could imagine similar scenes in which little French boys were squirming on the ground with laughter at solemn German officers whose Mercedes had broken down, during *their* Occupation.

After two hours we were towed back to Bonn. I decided to leave my driver to get the Humber repaired again while I made my way as best I could back to Duesseldorf. I managed once more to persuade the Transport Officer at Bonn to lend me, for the last time, one of the local cars. When I got to Duesseldorf I found I was even more helpless there without a car than I had been in Bonn. I had, for a day or two, to read, walk about, write letters and think.

Colonel D——, formerly a journalist, who had now joined the Mess, very kindly invited me to attend various conferences connected with the re-starting of the German Press, which were being held in towns in the Ruhr. This was useful to me, as apart from the interest of the conferences themselves, I was able to spend at least an hour or so looking into the question of libraries in each of the great Ruhr towns.

The first conference I attended was not in the Ruhr, but in Duesseldorf itself, and it was not to start a new paper, but to consider the problems of the *Rheinische Revue,* which was one of the very few papers already started under German editorship. The German editors were subdued, tired men, but they had a point of view which they contested strongly with the British officers. Dr. Vogel, the chief editor, insisted that he would like much more criticism from his readers to be allowed in the *Revue.* He complained that after Montgomery's declaration that a great measure of freedom of speech was going to be allowed to the Germans, his readers could not understand why their letters complaining, not about the Military Government but about the German Civilian Administration, were not published. He said that they were inclined to argue: "Montgomery approves of free speech. It must therefore not be the British but the German editors who are responsible for the censorship of opinion."

He was told that a greater measure of freedom would soon be allowed. Dr. Vogel then went on to point out that the Germans knew nothing whatever about the truth of the main events which had happened in Germany during the last ten or twelve years. For example, it would be interesting for Germans if, on the anniversary of the outbreak of war, there were revelations in the German Press of what had really happened in September 1939. Again, the greatest interest centred on the German leaders, Goering, Hess, etc. Why couldn't there be many more articles containing revelations about these men?

Here the British journalist officers disagreed. One of them, in particular, strongly took the line that news should be strictly new, that is to say, entirely contemporary, and that there should be no going back over the past. It was also pointed out that when reviews and books were published, Germany's recent past would be fully dealt with; and that in any case the Nuremburg Trials would provide Germans with news of the past activities of the Nazi leaders.

Dr. Vogel next said that the *Rheinische Revue* had been criticized for publishing much "vague cultural stuff." He vigorously defended this policy. We looked at some copies of the *Rheinische Revue* and "culture" was seen to consist for the most part of photographs of cows grazing on the bank of the Rhine and of sentimental poems about the Rhine. A pathetic note of Rheinish separatism ran through the cultural side of the *Revue*. There was also a serialized version of Joseph Conrad's *Typhoon* which had been taking up a large amount of space (for the *Rheinische Revue* appeared only once a week during the past three months). Everyone present deplored the presence of *Typhoon,* but no one was responsible for it. A brigadier in the vicinity had rung up the editorial offices and said that no decent paper should be without a "serial." He insisted that there should be such a feature in the *Rheinische Revue;* and accordingly *Typhoon* was put in as no one could think of anything else to print.

Dr. Vogel complained that in addition to the whims of local military gods, he was also at the mercy of the idea held by certain authoritative British journalists in Hamburg that the entire German Press should be altered in character. He disagreed with this policy. He said that he thought the Germans could best be re-educated by papers to which they were accustomed, and he said that they would never get to care for "tabloid journalism."

I had the strangest impression of the harassed life of a German newspaper editor from this conference. I did not feel at all able to take sides in the conflict between English and German ideas about how these newspapers should be run. On the whole, the English were reasonable, I thought. Perhaps even there was something in the idea that a new format should be created for the German newspaper which might well look less like a Lutheran tract printed in Gothic type.

During the next days I attended several conferences in the Ruhr towns, held for the purpose of starting local newspapers. The idea of these meetings was to form groups of men representing different political parties and confessions, who would publish a joint newspaper in each town. Each interest would have a certain amount of space in the newspaper for the purpose of representing its point of view.

Thus at Wuppertal the meeting consisted of a Social Democrat, a Communist, a Christian Democrat, a Centre Party man, an Evangelical Pastor, a Catholic, and the Mayor, together with one or two other people, the reasons for whose presence were not clear. The editor of the paper was supposed to be a man either belonging to no party or else prepared to undertake that he would sink his own party views and make the newspaper truly representative of every opinion.

Colonel D—— was an able chairman of these meetings. At Wuppertal he began by asking two or three of those present to explain what they had been doing since 1933. The Christian Democrat explained that before Hitler came to power he was a nationalist but that primarily he was concerned with the conviction that the State must be Christian. When the Nazis came to power, he thought that he might, by joining them, introduce a Christian influence into the movement. However, he found that the party was entirely opposed to Christian ideas, so he withdrew his application for membership before it was accepted. He then gave a long and rather lifeless account of his relationship with the party, to prove that he had been persecuted by the Nazis. Two or three other right-wing and centralist members of the group gave similar accounts of themselves. One of them made much of the fact that he had refused to haul down the Red-White-Black nationalist flag from his house when asked to do so, so that they had sent thirty men round to take it away from him. Only the Communist seemed completely uncompromised and to be in no sense forced to excuse himself for his record. He did not have to give any long account of himself as he had been entirely opposed to the Nazis throughout his career and had been sent to a concentration camp for many years. He said that the Communists honourably and in good faith supported democracy and that they would be loyal to the Occupying Powers. Colonel D—— asked me whether I would like to ask any questions. I was interested in the Communist so I asked him when the Communists intended to return to Communism and introduce features in their programme other than those of simply co-operating with the Occupying Forces. He said that he believed that "sooner or later" the struggle between capitalists and proletariat, which for the time being was overshadowed by the overwhelming conditions of defeat, would resume its classical form and then the Communists would again take part in the struggle for the freedom of the proletariat.

All the delegates looked worn and hungry except for two fat and comfortable-looking Roman Catholic priests who seemed to agree with everything that everyone said.

At the Wuppertal meeting everyone agreed to co-operate in producing the projected newspaper. In Essen there was almost complete disagreement. The Social Democrat said emphatically that his party would not agree to work with the printing firm which had been chosen, even though it might be the only surviving printing works in Essen. The Communist, Dr. Renner, who had been a refugee, anti-Fascist, imprisoned by the Vichy Government in France and later handed over to Hitler, pointed out, rather dryly, that a newspaper which was supposed to represent completely opposed points of view would represent no point of view.

11. Fire and Blood

THE HUMBER COMPLETELY RECOVERED, AND THE DRIVER turned up at Duesseldorf, so that we could continue our searches into the libraries of the Ruhr. He was in a very cheerful mood. He had a kit-bag made of goat's hide. He was also wearing a pair of German field boots which he had been lent by the cobbler who, for the price of a few cigarettes, was repairing his own shoes. He said these boots were far better than English ones and that he could get them for fifty cigarettes if he wished to do so.

The car went along fine to Bonn where we had lunch, on our way to Aachen, where I wished to see whether they had carried out my previous instructions about the library. Everything was in order in Aachen, and after viewing the library I went to tea at the Officers' Mess. We were late back from Aachen and it was dark as we drove through the outskirts of Cologne. We went over one bad hole in the road which caused a fearful bump. A mile or so farther on there was a dragging scraping noise on the left-hand side of the car. This increased greatly as we turned a rather sharp corner. We got out and found that the left front wheel was almost off. There were only two nuts left and the bolts were badly bent. We took a nut from another wheel, tightened the two other nuts and proceeded very slowly to Bonn.

I spent a day reading Ernst Jünger's novel *Feuer und Blut*. This novel, published in 1929 (the same year as Goebbels's *Michael*), is one of the best war books I have read, and also one of the most deeply repulsive. It describes one single dramatic event—the German attack of March 1918 as it affected one part of the German Army. The action of the novel is as beautifully organized and described as a fine piece of engineering. One never loses the shape, the hardness and the shine of it. The drama consists of the entry of human feelings into a strong automatic prearranged movement of material forward to the front and into action. Nothing could be better than the picture of the men as part of a machine performing an action, whose driving force comes from decisions outside their control —and yet they still have feelings.

For Jünger, modern war is the supreme occasion in which man discovers the mystery of his own existence, not apart from, but in relation to and in conflict with modern inventions, modern technique, modern industry. Only in war can modern humanity measure itself against the machines which it has created. Using the word "material" in the sense in which it is used in the phrase, a "war of material," one might say that the whole of modern civilization is a matter of "material." However, there is a deep malaise in our civilization, which is caused by the fact that in times of peace the spiritual life of our civilization is not related to its dependence on these modern "material" conditions. Yet at the back of the minds of the most spiritually developed individuals there is an uneasy, an embittered, or an evasive awareness that they are simply the products of material conditions, against which they can never measure themselves. They can never prove their inner independence of these conditions, nor do they know, on the other hand, how to exploit "material" fully as a means of realizing their own existence more completely.

War is the occasion on which man most fully exploits and enters into the struggle of material, and it is also the occasion in which he discovers that margin of his own courage, his own isolation, his own existence, which is not dependent on material. In war, he himself becomes the instrument of machinery, and machinery becomes the instrument of his will. This is the "mystique" which justifies war for Ernst Jünger; and war is justified as an end in itself; he has no feelings of pity for war's victims, almost no feelings about the righteousness of war. The whole novel *Feuer und Blut,* is a sustained vision of the realization by men of their own existence at the moment when they are most integrated within the power and most at the mercy of the conflict of the material resources of modern civilization.

In the western slope some narrow, partly shattered fox-holes have been dug, out of which from time to time a row of white faces appear, edged by the sharp lines of their steel helmets. These faces are very remarkable, pale, dirty, utterly exhausted; two days would suffice to pare away from them every trace of flesh. The cheek bones spring sharply outwards, and the contours of the bone of the nose can be seen under the skin. This gives them an unpleasant resemblance to skulls, an effect which is still further emphasized by the gloomy deeply-sunk eyes.

The men to whom these faces belong are completely inactive. They have time to make themselves acquainted with every single signal from the aviators. And they know also the meaning of these signals. They are the commands to a battery of heavy artillery which has its position in a ruined village. There above are the eyes and there below is the arm. And in monotonous rhythm, whose oscillations still do not last as long as a minute, clusters of grenades spit forwards, to burst in a thundering quartet of explosions. Sometimes they crash in front of the defile, sometimes behind it, sometimes in the very middle, so that it is filled with a stinging smoke of explosions. Like a monotonous punishment in Hell, this spectacle continues all day long in an apparently dead landscape, and is observed only by the eyes of those who are participators in it.

This is the material. Before the eyes there swim the extensive centres of industry, with huge pit-heads and with the glow of furnaces at night, factory workshops with driving belts and flashing ladles, mighty goods-yards with shining tracks, the storm of gaily-coloured signal lamps and the orderliness of white arc-lamps which illuminate the area with their geometric patterns. Yes, there behind the front-lines hammering and joining goes on in the hard workshops of a gigantic productivity and then the machines are rolled along the lines of communication to the front like a great total of achievement, concentrated strength, to be poured out for the purpose of destroying human beings. The battle is a fearful measuring of the productive power of one side against that of the other, and victory is the success of the competitor who knows how to produce the material more quickly and ruthlessly than the other. Here the age in which we live shows its other side. The domination of machines over men, of the slave over the lord becomes apparent, and a deep dissension, which even in time of peace began to shatter the industrial and commercial order, shows its deadly shape in the battles of this age. The style of a materialist race, and technique, celebrates a bloody triumph. Here a reckoning has to be paid of debts which seem to have been long postponed and forgotten, and if we have to "go in there" there must be good grounds for doing so. There would be a good reason, even though perhaps we had no such debts, since fate does not recognize personal responsibilities. It is above all such considerations.

Strange that together with the recollection of that first battle of material, I remember something else quite different, and in fact quite a small incident which seemed to have no significance in relation to this mighty impression. It was on the same evening, which closed down over the defile after that endless day, on which also the magic really first began. The firing on the horizon glared ever more densely on the horizon; its brilliance was reflected high in the clouds like spasms of pulsing blood. It formed a long dancing chain, and melted finally into a single glowing wall. What was the significance then of the activity of the single battery? Its blows went under with a tremendous noise, in a thousandfold poisonous hissing of the paths of projectiles, which wove together above our heads into a net with a narrow mesh, surrounding us with scalding surf, a single coherent element, like the fire of the Greeks. We no longer felt anxious, because this spectacle was of a grandeur which could be confronted by no human feelings. We waited because there was no doubt that this prodigious expenditure of material must be followed by throwing in the men. And then I saw that, next to me the ensign W——, a mere boy, bent down and seized a wineflask which had been brought forward to him that evening by the supplying troops and which should have been saved for the hot hours of the following afternoon. I saw him raise it to his lips, empty it at one long draught and laughingly throw it over the parapet. And I understood what this meant: he realized that he would not be able to drink it to-morrow. But in this simple action there lay a such daring courage and such a self-evident power of superiority, that I suddenly had the sensation of a great freedom, I felt that I would like to embrace him, and that at once I had become quite gay.

This we also learnt, this feeling that man is superior to material when he sets his own behaviour against it, and that no mass

The Student Aulach Again

and super-mass of external forces is thinkable which can destroy the resistance of a brave heart.

But in order to learn this it is necessary for a man first to identify himself with material, then to fight against still more material, and finally to be destroyed by material. In such a picture, there is very little room left for pity for the inhabitants of the landscape which has been turned into a scene from hell, in order that the German soldiers may measure their own existence against demoniac forces which they have invoked. Nor is there much room for a cause. The enemy is someone who surely must inevitably be struck down by a combination of material and a will for destruction which it is impossible to withstand.

One idea has occurred to all of us at the same moment: that the enemy will be struck to the ground by one mighty blow. Our storm of fire is so overpowering and elemental, that it is impossible to imagine any strength capable of resisting it. And this idea fills us with a wild joy. We squeeze ourselves out of our dug-outs, out of our security, on which formerly we laid so much worth, and we dance around the trenches in the flickering light, like spirits possessed. Yes, we are possessed, possessed by an over-powering will, which becomes revealed in this landscape of fire, and we can no longer care about our own safety, whether we wish to do so or not.

Of course, the terrible shock is that there is another will even more overpowering and material even more overpowering than their own will to destroy. The "Ungluck," when it arrives, is incredible, because it destroys the faith in evil which knows that it can move mountains. Demoniacally possessed men with enormous material resources and complete confidence in themselves are confronted by a stubborn reality which refuses to bend to their will, and, indeed, flings them back and destroys them. With Herr Jünger the cry of "the way of the world is a hard and bitter one," comes quite sincerely from his heart, although he himself has nothing but approval for those who have given their lives to make it still harder and more bitter: those who, having created their landscape of blood and fire, are able to think:

Are not the landscapes which await us, then impossible and fabulous? No poet in his dreams has looked upon these burning fields. There are iron fields of craters, deserts with fiery islands of palm-trees, rolling walls made of fire and steel and plains of the dead, over which red storms drive. Flocks of steel birds swarm through the sky, and armoured machines plunge over the fields. And everything which causes feeling, from appalling physical pain to the uttermost joy of victory, is melted together here into a burning unity, to a picture of life itself blazing like lightning. Song, prayer, rejoicing, cursing and weeping—what more can we wish?

Perhaps one poet did dream of such a landscape: Milton, when he entered the feelings of Satan, cast forth from heaven, arriving in his own self-created hell, and saying:

> Hail horrors, hail
> Infernal world, and thou profoundest Hell
> Receive thy new Possessor: One who brings
> A mind not to be changed by Place or Time.
> The mind is its own place, and in itself
> Can make a Heav'n of Hell, a Hell of Heav'n.

12. The Student Aulach Again

ONE MORNING WHILE I WAS STILL DELAYED AT BONN, I MET the student, Aulach, again, and went for a walk with him. He was still negotiating to go abroad and to cease to be a German. He was well informed about the Germans, since he works with them all the time as one of them, and they say things to him which they would say to no foreigner. He said that the Nazis are getting quite cheeky, though he does not think they represent a serious movement. Their line is to put the worst interpretation on everything we do. For instance, if we send food to Germany, they say that we are only doing it so as to keep the workers just alive while they are working to enable us to take far more away from Germany than we are sending in. He said we are cutting down a lot of wood, but that the idea that we are systematically deforesting Germany is grossly exaggerated.

Aulach said that he would take me to his favourite hideout in Bonn which is a deserted landing-stage on the Rhine. While we were walking there—through all the dust and ruins of the deserted area of the town near the river—he said that he hated these ruins of Germany. "I have no connection with them. They are not MY ruins which have been taken away from me personally, nor am I in the slightest degree interested in reconstructing them."

We got to the landing-stage, which was very pleasant. Here you can certainly lie down on a little peninsula formed by the float of the landing-stage projecting into the Rhine, blown over by fresh breezes and surrounded by running waters which wash away the humid stinging scent of the whole of Bonn. It is quite extraordinary the sense of difference. Aulach said that he comes here often. Sometimes he lies here alone at night until two or three in the morning. What thoughts must be chasing through his handsome, bony, solitary, defiant, intelligent rather mad head. Aulach is significant, not because he is in any way "typical," but because he is one spirit thinking and brooding in this post-war Germany, just as after the last war there were the Nazis thinking their nihilistic thoughts. The Germans are very cerebral, but for the most part they are a cerebral mass seething with apathetic sullen ideas. Aulach is in a state of ferment, highly infectious to the German passively cerebrating mass, filled with its dull sense of injury, self-pity, cruelty, bitterness and potential fury.

I told him that I had just read Ernst Jünger's *Feuer und Blut* and Goebbels's novel, *Michael*. Aulach said that Jünger wasn't merely a nationalist writer, he was also regarded with some favour by the communists, because he expressed a ferocious radicalism which, being essentially anti-bourgeois, was a meeting-place of the nationalist and communist ideas. I said that Jünger was diabolic and that *Feuer und Blut* was a masterpiece written from the depths of an experience of hell. Aulach said: "I cannot disapprove of that. Jünger is a devil. And I have so much understanding of devils that I do not condemn diabolic books at all."

When he said this I felt a strange and exciting sympathy for him. "What do you mean by a devil?" I asked. "A devil is a person who is aware of himself as a unique part of existence. To him the fact that he exists and that he is a part of the human condition of existing is more important than society and than the whole world. Most people consider themselves part of their social environment, their job, their class, etc. They do not think much about the fact that they exist. Therefore a devil is quite *outside* his environment. A devil despises in his heart the whole social and political structure of our time. He realizes that democracy is just as bad as fascism for example; or that if there is any difference, that perhaps it is just 1 per cent better, and this is so little that it is not worth arguing about. Anyway, the whole conflict as it is presented to us in the form of a struggle between external political systems is unreal to him. If anything about it is real, it is the fact of the struggle itself—the violence, the hatred, the destruction, the chaos which it involves."

Aulach said that he despised the Nazis, because they were not honest devils. He said that there was a diabolic side of Hitler which he admired because Hitler really saw through the sham of bourgeois society. But at the same time Hitler was not honest with himself, nor was he true to his friends. "A true devil recognizes in the world a few other devils, people who despise all the fixed forms of society. They are willing to destroy all the outward political forms in order to intensify the sensation in themselves of their own state of being. They will put towns and even whole countries to the sword, but they remain true to themselves and loyal to each other. A true devil regards the majority of human beings as just outward external institutions to be no more respected than a city company or a society for the protection of animals. But the test of the true devil is that he is loyal to other devils. The Nazis failed by this test."

I said that I was ten years older than he and that although I certainly shared the experience of a sensation which he was talking about, I did not believe that the whole of society should be sacrificed to the contempt of a few people who, justifiably or unjustifiably, believe themselves to be more authentic than other people. Suffering was also real—even the suffering of dishonest people and of people lacking in the genius to be honest with themselves—and it was the duty of people who realize the vanity of most human aims and institutions nevertheless to mitigate horror and suffering.

Aulach had no sympathy with this point of view. He said: "I have noticed in your poems, which you showed me, that you sometimes write simply of the experience of being alive and of your own intimate experience of yourself as an individual isolated within the universe. When you write in this way you are filled with social despair, and you have no religious or political beliefs whatever. Directly, out of a sense of conscience, you try to introduce a constructive idea into your writing, you fail."

"All the same," I said, "one must look for a constructive idea. If one has the sense of despair and of evil, then one must look for the sense of hope and of good with which to confront despair and evil."

"There are no such alternatives as good and evil. There is only truth and untruth. Truth is diabolic and energetic and destructive. What is called good is only a façade of untruths. All social aims of democracy, and progress and reconstruction and re-education, which you talk about, seek to establish a kind of routine, on the false assumption that there is something concrete and enduring in nations, parties, businesses and machinery which can absorb people's lives and make them think of themselves as parts of a structure which has nothing to do with the innermost reality of their existence. All talk of right and wrong is an attempt to make one loyal to something outside the truth about oneself—which is that one is alive and is going to die and that one has no loyalty to anyone except oneself."

After this I had to go back to the Transit Mess. Aulach walked back with me. En route he said: "Recently I have written an essay on the significance of the atom bomb." "What is significant about it?" I asked. "It is very significant that 90 per cent of the scientists who invented it were Jews. We are not grateful to the Jews enough. The atom bomb is the final culmination of the Jewish analytic and destructive genius which can create nothing but only destroy. It will result in the Third World War which will complete the unfinished task of this war." "What is that?" "Destroy the whole of this unnatural, decadent civilization of great cities and false values. After that, among the ruins of our civilization, a new civilization of people who have renounced our materialism for ever, will grow."

We talked also a bit about psychoanalysis. Aulach said that psychoanalysts were "devils on a very low stratum of intelligence." It was characteristic, he added, that most of them were Jews. They realized that the innermost being of the individual was more important than the social structure but they interpreted this being entirely on the sexual level, which was of slight importance. What was important was the whole condition of existence of which sex was only a small part.

13. Ernst Jünger

A DAY OR TWO AFTER THIS CONVERSATION WITH AULACH, MY car had recovered again and we went to Hanover. There was only one slight mishap on the way: a puncture, when we were half an hour outside the town. Directly the car was punctured it became dark very rapidly, and this was rather awkward, especially as we had stopped almost under a bridge. We had plenty of opportunity to observe the roadsense of people driving under this bridge, by those who nearly ran into us. American drivers of jeeps seemed on the whole to be the least careful.

On the way to Hanover I called for a last few minutes each at the libraries of Dortmund, Bochum and Essen. I began to feel rather depressed about my library job, as owing to the breakdown of transport my researches had been far from thorough and my statistics were far from complete. Indeed there had been whole days in which I had forgotten all about libraries. Of course, the reason for this had been the breakdown of the Humber. Yet, somehow, this did not seem altogether convincing. Sometimes, also, the library job seemed to me quite absurd; the libraries were practically capable of opening themselves without any intervention on my part. Everything that I was supposed to do such as "screening" the librarians and their books, the local Military Government authorities could obviously do much better. Besides this, I could never make up my mind whether I approved of the policy of "purging" libraries of Nazi books. In a sense it seemed to me very unimportant because it was only justified by the fact that it was impossible to carry out thoroughly: I mean, really to burn or destroy or completely take away the Nazi books from the Germans would have been a wrong policy, but luckily it was an impossible one to carry out. Since it was not possible, all it amounted to was taking some Nazi books off the shelves and putting them somewhere else, and this only seemed desirable in a very general and vague way which I could not feel strongly about.

My driver was rather sad at leaving the girl with whom he had had the platonic relationship in Bonn. He had got on well not only with her, but with her family. He said: "The thing that makes me laugh about them is that I can never do anything wrong as far as they're concerned. Everything I do is right with them. I have never had that happen before." As he can't speak a word of German, nor she English, it's extraordinary how they get themselves across to each other. She seemed to spend her time largely in tears at my driver's imminent departure, usually made less imminent by the vagaries of the Humber.

While we were in Dortmund I went to see the Oberbürgermeister for a few minutes. When I came back to the car, I found that my driver had two cigars. He explained to me that he had got these in exchange for one cigarette, which seemed to me an extraordinary black market deal. The Oberbürgermeister told me that they had introduced a rule in Dortmund that nothing whatever must be built. This was their first step in reconstruction. The reason for it was that so many millions of marks damage had been done to the system of pipes, drains and wires running under the city that they could not make any overground alterations until they had decided how far it was possible to restore these underground systems.

The utter desolation of Dortmund depressed me for most of the day, while we drove through the beautiful country. As we approached Hanover it was evening and the ripe fields glowed under a greying sky, as though they had absorbed all the light of the day, like a sponge, and were now exhaling it to the dusk. Owing to the puncture it was well after dinner when we found the Information Control Unit, where we were politely welcomed, though unexpected.

The next day there was difficulty in replacing the inner tube of my car, which had been so badly punctured as to be useless. I sat about most of the day waiting, not knowing where to go as I was sharing a room with an officer and all the sitting rooms were being cleaned. It was very cold. I read a copy of *Palgrave's Golden Treasury* and was very astonished by Wordsworth's *Ruth, or the Influences of Nature*. This suddenly appeared to me as a poem in which the poet has revealed far more of himself than he has meant to reveal. In fact, to use the student Aulach's language, Wordsworth in this poem is fascinated by the devil. He is completely carried away by his own fantasy of the vice-ridden

> Youth from Georgia's shore—
> A military casque he wore
> With splendid feathers drest;
> He brought them from the Cherokees;

> The feathers nodded in the breeze
> And made a gallant crest.
>
> The youth of green savannahs spake,
> And many an endless, endless lake
> With all its fairy crowds
> Of islands, that together lie
> As quietly as spots of sky
> Among the evening clouds.
>
> Nor less, to feed voluptuous thought,
> The beauteous forms of Nature wrought—
> Fair trees and gorgeous flowers;
> The breezes their own languor lent;
> The stars had feelings, which they sent
> Into those favoured bowers.

This is not just romanticism. It is the language of ecstasy, which is something quite different. It is the language of a fantastic and tempting condition of experience for the achievement of which everything else is sacrificed—as a drunkard sacrifices everyone, including himself, to achieve his drunkenness. Such language is rare, but it is not confined to the romantics. I feel it sometimes in *Comus,* for example.

In the afternoon I had to decide that it was too late to get to Hamburg, as the car was not ready till four-thirty. Then I remembered that I had a note in my pocket from someone in Paris for Ernst Jünger, who lives only twenty minutes from here. Accordingly I got into the car and went to his house. This was a charming parsonage, built in farmhouse style, and standing next to a church. I was shown into a comfortable room with leathern armchairs and lined with beautiful books. Herr Jünger came down and welcomed me. He read the letter. While he did so I watched him. He is smallish, dressed in comfortable tweeds, with the kind of tanned, lined active expression under a head of grey hair, which one sees in countrymen who do not age with the years. He has a thin tight mouth, with lines round it which make one think of a whip.

He said: "I have two friends upstairs who have come to see me. Would you mind joining us?"

The two friends were a Herr B—— von K—— and a Herr Weimann, who is, I believe, a dramatist. B—— von K—— had cold grey eyes, a pale salmon-colour complexion, sandy hair, a well-formed mouth and a gaze of extraordinary steadiness. Weimann was swarthy and dark-haired; a leathern, wrinkled, kind face like that of a mountain guide. There was also a woman there whom I took (perhaps wrongly) to be Frau Jünger.

They were all seated round a table on which there was coffee, some cake resembling bread and some slices of bread covered thinly with a meat paste. There was a fire in the room, which was pleasantly warm.

Jünger asked me if I was going to Paris again. I said yes, so then he said that there were one or two people to whom he would like to send messages of greeting. He mentioned the names of several French writers to whom he wished to be remembered.

I said that it was unlikely that I should see Montherlant (one of these writers) as he was considered to be somewhat compromised by his behaviour during the Occupation. I said that I did not know what to think about this myself, but that out of respect for the attitude of my French friends I did not try to see people in the position of Montherlant. Jünger said rather impatiently: "That is a childishness which the French must get over. They must really learn to be a little more reasonable, and to adopt a maturer attitude about these things." I was rather surprised when Jünger went on talking expansively and confidently about the French, as though he expected to be back in Paris quite soon. This attitude was in very striking contrast to that of most intelligent Germans who seem to have resigned themselves to the fact that it will be impossible for them to travel with dignity for many years.

The conversation became more general, but probably I had Herr Jünger's remarks about France in mind when I said that unfortunately the Nazis had left Germany the legacy of being hated which would have the effect of isolating her. Jünger said that he agreed about this, but he pointed out that if we hated Germany that would mean that the legacy of the Nazis was to the rest of Europe as well as to Germany, in making the other European nations hate Germany as Germany has hated the Jews.

I said that I myself was opposed to the isolation of Germany. After the last war, I went on, she had become too isolated, particularly in her culture, which might have become Europeanized. Indeed, the writers and all the artists showed a desire to become international, in which they were not given sufficient strength and help from foreign countries. Instead of producing a strong European cultural movement in Germany after the last war, there had been a weak and rather decadent one which finally produced a reaction towards German nationalism even in culture itself.

They asked me how I thought German culture might become incorporated into and strengthened by the rest of Europe after this war. I said that later on I would like to see an International Review for Europe, on the very highest level, in which the best German writers were published side by side with English and French ones, and perhaps with Russian ones also. In this Review, the German questions which concerned the whole of Europe, such as German philosophy, German ideas about power, German history, etc, together with other European questions might be discussed very seriously and with equal frankness by thinkers of all nations, since they would be on a level which was human and not immediately controversial. In this way the German writers would be more or less absorbed into the whole European movement and also they would be confronted with European critical standards. One of the bad things after the last war was the low standard of critical thought in Germany and the lack of relation of German achievements in such things as expressionism, to achievements in France, America and England. Jünger was enthusiastic about this idea and said that such a Review should be trilingual—printed in all three languages. He said that a great opportunity now offered because Germany was in the mood to accept a lead from abroad. I said that this might be true from the point of view of Germany, but that perhaps the rest of Europe was not so ready to collaborate with Germany. Although there were a few Englishmen and Frenchmen who were willing immediately to enter into intellectual relations with Germans, I thought it might be very wise to respect the deep feelings of ordinary people who had suffered the most outrageous wrongs as the result of actions done by Germans. We must wait and be patient, realizing that finally Germany must become part of the European family.

B—— von K—— said that he was entirely agreed with this. He himself was concerned with a reorientation of German youth towards religious values within a new youth movement.

I said that I thought that one of the things that would most help other peoples to understand Germany would be if there were some recognition amongst Germans of German guilt. I did not think, though, the guilt should be charged against the whole German people on the assumption that they were all equally guilty for all crimes. Guilt was not so much a general accusation as a general question which ought to be raised. It was a question of when and where and how and to what degree individual Germans were guilty rather than of all Germans being guilty.

Jünger: "Yes, but it depends also in what form you expect us to admit our guilt and what action you intend to take when we do admit it. We can't admit it if you put it in the form of 'You're guilty, so I'm entitled to take your wallet from you.' "

Weimann: "We should talk less about *the* Germans, *the* English, *the* French, etc. Rather, every German should ask himself in his own conscience whether he is not responsible for some of the crimes of the Nazis—even if he has never heard of Belsen and Buchenwald."

He was silent for a moment, then he went on: "It may appear to you, as an Englishman now travelling in Germany, that the Germans will not admit to the English that plea of guilt which the English demand for all these mass graves you discover. But during the raids on Berlin I often slept in public shelters, and I was amazed how, time and again, the ordinary Berliners in their *Bunkers* said, as they heard the bombs falling: 'This is what we have asked for. This is how we acted towards the Jews and this is now being visited against us.' "

They all agreed that during the later part of the war Germans had truly realized the disaster which they had brought upon themselves. "In a way," said Weimann, "there are advantages in living amongst all these ruins. Although it is nice to have possessions, one is freer without them. Now we are free, we have the possibility of spiritual revival."

Frau Jünger (?) said that Hitler had one great point in his favour, and that was the injustice of the Treaty of Versailles. I said if this was so, the same thing might well happen again.

Many harsh things were happening in Germany and many more were bound to happen: if Germans chose to consider them as "injustices" without relating them to the causes which had produced these things then they would build up another great national grievance.

Jünger: "Exactly. But one must draw a line somewhere. We must stop all this hatred now, once and for all."

After this, I had to go and Jünger showed me downstairs and through the garden to my car. While we were alone I said: "I have read recently your novel *Feuer und Blut*. I think it is a masterpiece, but at the same time it seemed to me very shocking. It looks on war as the only aim in modern life." Jünger said: "That is so, but it is real. It is about something extremely important to me, one of the realest things in my life." He mentioned that he had won two of the highest medals for bravery in the last war, and in this war another very high medal but this time for saving someone's life. "Have you changed your point of view since you wrote *Feuer und Blut?*" I asked.

"Certainly, I have done so. But all that was a necessary stage of my experiences. At twenty a man is a warrior: and I was twenty then."

14. Hamburg

THE NEXT DAY I LEFT HANOVER FOR HAMBURG, STOPPING FOR a moment at Kirchhorst to take a photograph of Herr Jünger. He was friendly and seemed pleased to be photographed. I also asked him to sign my copy of *Auf den Marmorklippen*, his novel which has been interpreted as a satire on the Nazis. I did not tell him that I had been given this by the librarian of the public library of Aachen, because she did not know whether to keep it on the shelves and because she had more copies than she knew how to deal with.

Outside Zelle the car developed its old primordial trouble of spitting and "cutting out." The driver cleaned out the carburettor and then it went again but rather badly, at not more than 40 m.p.h. I seem to have acquired a whole philosophy of life from this Humber. From it I have learned that it does not really matter whether I arrive at my goal at the expected time, that I can miss meals and engagements, that I must be patient and that often the vacuum produced in my life by a delayed journey may lead to meetings of the greatest interest. The pages of this journal have been guided, not by my own will but by the obstinacy of the Humber which kept me for many days in Bonn when I should have been compiling statistics about libraries in the Ruhr.

We motored slowly through a country of clustered spearforests and gloomy heaths. Every few miles we passed wrecks of tanks and cars along the side of the roads. Occasionally there were great aluminium corpses of crashed aeroplanes lying in the fields, and there were many graves, often graves of German pilots surrounded by fragments of the wrecks of their fighters.

We arrived at Hamburg at about 2 P.M., too late for my driver to have lunch at his Mess, but just in time for me to have it at mine. The Atlantic Hotel is, outside the Officers' Club in Paris, the most grandiose Mess for officers I have ever been to. It also contains very grandiose-looking officers.

The first person I ran into was a Jewish refugee friend who was visiting Germany to make a report on conditions in the Universities. The return to Germany had evidently shaken him a great deal. He said that, for one thing, he had never been so conscious of being a Jew. He thought that on the whole those who followed the teaching of the Old Testament proved juster than those who followed that of the New. He had realized during the past days the meaning of "an eye for an eye, a tooth for a tooth." This stern injunction had been replaced by the noble Christian admonition to "turn the other cheek." But the Jewish law could be observed. An eye for an eye, and a tooth for a tooth could be exacted, and then charity could begin. Christianity with its idealer precepts never knew where to stop. Instead of searching for the real authors of the crimes and then punishing them with remorseless Jewish justice, we made a whole nation be punished.

My refugee friend seemed as depressed by the Germans as by the Occupying Forces. He said that on the previous evening he had paid a visit to a charming and sympathetic German family, mostly of young people. They all said that the Belsen Trials were propaganda and that the alleged crimes of Kramer, etc., were humanly impossible.

He said when we prepared the Belsen Trials, we thought the effect of democratic justice would be to convince the Germans that we really stood for an impartial examination of all the evidence, the hearing of the defence, etc. But it had not had this effect at all. The majority of Germans believed that the trials were a put-up job and that they were only being prolonged because the accused had so much to be said on their side that we could not entirely repress their evidence—as the Nazis could not entirely repress the defence of the Reichstag Trial. They thought that we were fumbling in our methods of staged trials as the Nazis had also fumbled when they first seized power. These Germans said that if the accused were really guilty, and if we knew they were, why didn't we dispose of the whole matter quickly and condemn them?

Fortunately some of the stories he told me about individual Germans were more encouraging than this. For example, he had visited an institute for lunatics run by a certain von B—— who had resisted all the attempts of the Nazis to use his lunatics for scientific experiments. My friend had asked him how he had managed to hold out against the pressure of the S.S. This man, of saintly appearance, with a long white beard, had replied: "God built very high walls around our institution and protected us. We simply refused." Then he added: "We made the mistake of hating the S.S. too much. They were very pitiable people, and we should have loved and prayed for them much more."

Another person I met in the Mess at Hamburg was Boyman, the film man. He was in a very ebullient mood after dinner one evening: "Boy, what a day! Boy, what shots!" he said at the end of what was certainly one of the most beautiful days I have known even in Hamburg. According to him, everything in Germany was marvellous. The Military were doing a tremendous job. I asked him what he meant by this, and he said: "Look at the traffic. Look at the signs. Look at the wires for the telephone system," he added. He had been to Berlin. He said that the looting and raping and shooting by the Russians were "grossly exaggerated," mostly by the *Daily Telegraph* and other anti-Russian sources.

It was difficult to argue about this. What does "grossly exaggerated" mean, anyway? Obviously anything that happens and which causes a sensation, is in a sense, grossly exaggerated. It is all a question, I suppose, of whether or not one cares. I cannot carry on this kind of argument. Perhaps I exaggerate, but the homelessness of thousands of people, the ruins, the refugees, the distress, the hunger, haunt me, and since I have no statistical picture in my mind I do not even know whether I do exaggerate.

Boyman also said that he did not think that many thousands of people would starve to death this year in Berlin. He said that he had this on the authority of the Oberbürgermeister. He said that he thought that a few thousands might die in the camps of Displaced Persons, but he did not seem to think that this was a relevant factor (if he were a German, for the same statistical reasons, presumably he would not think Belsen a relevant factor).

The conversation got on to Russian Democracy versus Western Democracy (an unprofitable subject). Boyman said that we had in England a limited measure of political democracy. The Russians have "economic democracy." Also he made much of the fact that the Russians have the great freedom of being able to recall a deputy who is not satisfactory. This power of recall was tremendously important, he said, and it showed how much more democratic the Soviet Parliament was than our own, in some ways.

He said also that the Russians were far more "individualist" that we were. "What could be more ridiculous than to say they are not individualists and then to complain about their looting?" he asked. "Isn't it what we're complaining about, the fact that they behave with a great deal more individual liberty than our troops do? They get out of control of their own officers, and then we say that they are not individualists! It is we who lack the freedom of individual behaviour."

I found it very difficult to compare the two systems. Thinking it over afterwards, it seemed to me that the difference might be between the amounts of terror employed by the central governing authority. Terror means violent suppression of the rights of individual self-expression. Every legal system is to some extent a form of terrorization, but in England this terror is carried on publicly and within legal forms which everyone recognizes. There is comparatively little political terror. In Russia there is certainly more terror and it is vaguer in application and it takes a political form. Freedom of speech and of writing in England is evidence that there is no terror directed against such freedom. Lack of such freedom in Russia is indirect evidence of a background of terror. In so far as we have exercised political terror against freedom of opinion (in India, for example), the British Empire is directly comparable with Russia.

Now, political terror is a matter of indifference with people like Boyman. They take the line that for the State to own and administer all the means of production is "economic democrary" and therefore freedom of opinion seems to them unimportant. It is impossible to argue about this, because one either thinks that freedom of opinion is all-important or one doesn't. But a glance at the present conditions of Central Europe makes one think that it may be important.

I had a bedroom in the Atlantic Hotel which had three beds in it. On the first night I slept alone there. On the second night an American Jew and a New Zealander occupied the two other beds. Before the New Zealander arrived the American Jew had a long business conversation with the Polish Jew who had come up to the comparative privacy of our *chambre à trois* for the purpose. It was about a book which someone had almost finished writing about Belsen, of which the American had the manuscript. He said that it must be completed and published immediately or "no one would be interested." The Polish Jew said: "Oh, but surely people will still care in a few months time?" The American said consideringly: "Well, maybe it might always have a certain slight historic interest, but no one will want to read about all that in six months from now."

It is extraordinary how New Zealanders and Australians

remain cockneys. It makes one think twice about "re-educating" the Germans. One would have thought that by now their great open spaces, their mountains, their waterfalls, their lakes and their antipodesian Burgundy would have "re-educated" them. But not at all.

In the morning the American woke at 5.50 A.M., with a great roar, was called at 6.0 A.M., and explained that he was already awake, was telephoned at 6.10 A.M., and had his boots brought at 6.15 A.M. The New Zealander woke up at 7 A.M., got up, massaged his hair very slowly, breathing out all the time very heavily from his lungs, without apparently ever taking any air in. One would expect anyone brought up in the great spaces to breathe in huge gusts of wonderful air. But this Kiwi still had the Londoner's habit of expelling a loathsome foggy atmosphere from a thick chest.

The centre of Hamburg was patched up and not badly damaged. I stayed in the centre built round Lake Alster, avoiding the huge dock areas, San Pauli, and so on, and trying to recapture something of the mood of the Hamburg which I knew in the summer and autumn of 1929. On a fine day, Hamburg is one of the most beautiful cities in Europe. The lake was the most wonderful colour all this week: a dazzling blue with a silky softness which made it seem a pool of sky with wings of white sails drifting gently through it. The nights were even more beautiful with a starry sky above a wedge of silhouetted houses gleaming like black jet with hard lights set in them, and then the Plough reflected among reflected lights, plunged into the soft web of the lake.

I had promised Herr B—— von K—— whom I had met with Herr Jünger, that I would call on him in the suburb near Hamburg where he lived. I did so one afternoon. This suburb, called Oltmarschen, consists of houses, each of which seems almost lost in surrounding woods and green fields. One never has a view of more than two or three houses at a time. Here I took tea with B—— von K——, Weimann, and Herr and Frau Ellbrechter, von K——'s hosts.

Von K—— said that ever since I had last spoken to him he had been thinking of some remark I had let fall about the necessity of Germans becoming Europeans. He said: "Perhaps you are quite right. Now, in the last seventy years, Germany has involved Europe in three wars which have resulted in the ruin of a great part of Europe. Perhaps we should abandon the idea of a German nation altogether. We have proved ourselves incapable of taking our place in Europe, and instead of creating we have destroyed. All the same, if we give up the idea of Germany, as Germans we still exist. And what we ask of you is some hope that in five or in ten or in fifteen years, as men and women, we may take our place on equal terms with the men and women of the rest of the continent."

He said that for three years he had fought on the Eastern Front. He had seen enough to convince him that the Russians were completely justified in taking everything that they wanted from the Germans. "I myself have lost absolutely everything," he said. "I had large estates in East Prussia, and everything I possessed was there. I now live in two rooms with my wife and three children. But all that is quite right. In fact it gives me a sense of liberation and even of happiness to feel that I can start my life again, after what I have seen. Really, nothing else except this radical change in my own circumstances would have offered me the hope that perhaps I may do something to help make a new Europe."

I asked him what he had seen, and he said it would be too difficult to say. "Doubtless, though," he went on, "you have heard of the tremendous destruction, and you have also heard of things which I myself did not know about, but which I do not doubt, such as Belsen and Buchenwald. These things justify any amount of recompense. Let the Russians take everything they want. Let them strip the factories of their machines, and the houses down to the smallest gadgets, such as electric switches. We should not complain about that. In fact, we should be glad to do everything we can by way of recompense. But all the same, certain things are required if there is to be any future in which we can ultimately play a constructive part. One is that there should not be any Buchenwalds and Belsens under your Occupation. Of course, from a certain point of view, even that would be justified, but all the same if thousands or more people starved and were killed in camps now, I cannot see there ever being an end to the hatred which has been begun by us. So confine your revenge to the real criminals who are responsible for the German Camps, and recompense yourselves by taking as much of our property as you want. But do not do what we have done."

I asked him whether he knew of there being any camps on our side.

"They can take all our property in East Prussia," he said, "but when I hear of thousands of people being driven out in herds, with nowhere to live, and when I hear of many other such things, I begin to fear that you may wake up one morning perhaps two or three years from now, and suddenly realize, as we have realized, that there is the weight of the murder of thousands of people on your conscience. And you will then feel perhaps as I feel to-day that, although you knew almost nothing about what was going on, you are nevertheless not without responsibility.

"Another point," he went on, "is that we cannot know where we are in Germany, unless you have a policy. It is not just a question of whether you are severe or not, but of lines of action being defined beyond which we can have confidence that you won't go. It would be far better to make very severe terms and stick to them than to make no terms at all and then perhaps behave with unexpected mildness. Because what really matters is not your mildness or your severity, but whether you enable us to live in the light of certainty or condemn us to the perpetual fog of apprehension."

He said that he believed it was possible to bring together in Germany the people who still believed in Christian principles of conduct. He thought that Germany was capable of religious revival, but that this would only be achieved by the devotion of individuals.

When the British had first arrived in Germany, he said, many people had looked to them as saviours. Now there was a certain feeling of disappointment about us. I said that we were merely human: and that it was an inevitable psychological misunderstanding that the Germans should expect us either to be devils or else perfect. I pointed out that to some extent the English had also had this attitude towards the German refugees who had come to England. Many people were prepared to help them, on the condition that they behaved like martyrs and saints. But then, when the refugees turned out to be humans with the faults of humans, those people who had at first helped them had an excuse for not continuing to do so. In the same way, by expecting the British to be saviours, the Germans now had an excuse for pretending to be disappointed when they discovered that we were mere human beings.

Von K—— smiled and agreed that the situation was inevitable. I asked what specific forms the sense of disappointment took. Frau Ellbrechter immediately answered, quoting examples of furniture being burnt, women raped, medals torn off the uniforms of officers, etc. Von K—— said that such incidents were inevitable, and he did not think they greatly mattered. What mattered more was an easy-going attitude towards the Nazis, together with a distrustful attitude towards those Germans who were really trying to work well with the Allies. For example, he himself was responsible in a certain *Kreis* for organizing education. The Military Government authorities would not allow him to select teachers who had been officers or non-commissioned officers in the army. This meant that he could not provide the staff necessary to carry on with the teaching.

He said that it would be much better if the Military Government trusted him to choose his teachers. They could say to him: "If you fail us and select Nazi teachers, then you will be shot." He was sure that if he were given that amount of freedom and confidence his teachers would not let him down; nor would he let the Allies down.

I was rather amused at his telling me of the difficulties in finding teachers, because his argument had been aptly illustrated for me by meeting two schoolchildren a few yards from the Ellbrechters' front door just before I called. As I was a few minutes early, I talked to these children, whom I saw staring at me with curiosity. They said: "At our school we learn Latin and Biology." "Don't you learn anything else?" I asked. "No," they replied. "You see, the History, Geography, English and Mathematics teachers have all been purged."

Von K—— said that in the formation of the new Germany some of the army officers must play a part because they included the best minds in the country. People who had evaded the war were not necessarily the best friends of democracy, and had not necessarily done so because they were democrats. He said that he himself had been an officer, had commanded a regiment, and it had given him pride and happiness to have the confidence of his men. The fact, of course, that he was an officer shows that there are exceptions in our rule of not making use of officers.

Von K—— gave an impression of manliness, straightforwardness and responsibility, which seemed extraordinary in Germany to-day. In a simple and direct way he had accepted his position, and he was doing his utmost to work with the British. He was also forming around him a group of people who were agreed on the same necessity of "starting from zero." The idea of this group did not give me quite the same confidence as he did himself. He came from an old and world-famous family, and however good his intentions might be, it seemed that he would have to be very acute and clever, as well as honest and self-sacrificing to free himself from the old Prussian nationalist influences.

A few days after meeting him in Hamburg, I visited him at the house near Bunde, where, with many other evacuated families, his family was living. He invited me to share the very simple meal, consisting of a soup followed by potatoes, which he had with his family. After the meal we went for a walk, and he talked once more of his belief that a few outstanding individuals in Germany could do a great deal to influence the country to co-operate with the rest of Europe and of his faith in German youth. He showed me a collection of poems which he had made from manuscripts handed round by soldiers during the war. They were all of a sentimental, rather pathetic, nature. He also showed me an article he had written, under the title, *Thoughts on the Theme: Why Have We Lost the War?* This article was expressed most uncompromisingly. In effect, what it did was to confront the evil in contemporary Germany, expressed in the starkest and most recognizable terms, and not shrinking from references to the concentration camps and lying propaganda, with the good:

> Recent years and this cruel war have brought nearly all those things which we hold for firm and sacred into danger of collapse: truth and humanity, reason and right. We lived in a possessed world. For many of us the result was not unexpected when the insanity of a day broke out into a delirium in which this poor European humanity sank back, fanatical, stupefied and mad.
>
> On the other hand, there has perhaps never been a time when people were so inwardly prepared and so acquainted with the problem of co-operating to save their country and their culture. Many people have seen very clearly the increasing political and spiritual destruction of the last years. Amongst still more the complete collapse at the end of the war, which now leaves its marks bitterly on their own bodies, has prepared the ground for such thoughts. For the majority of human beings are more sensitive physically than spiritually.
>
> Moreover, a great part of the German people is ready to-day to take upon themselves the guilt for what has happened. And is this sense of guilt not an ethical value in itself which gives hope and which may lead to a new beginning?

The document ended with an appeal for a return to Christian values and to the Churches.

15. Berlin

ONE DAY WHEN I WAS AT THE ATLANTIC HOTEL AT HAMBURG, there was a message to say that my wife was giving some concerts (she is Natasha Litvin, the pianist) for the R.A.F. Malcolm Clubs in Germany. As my work ended with the visit to Hamburg I joined her in visiting Hildesheim, Bückeburg, Zelle and various other places where she played. These arrangements meant a fairly complete break in my German impressions. The R.A.F. lead a kind of life which is very isolated from that of all the other forces administering Germany. They live in their huge compounds taken over from the Luftwaffe, they talk their peculiar, highly-developed slang and they bring with them always the sense that they belong to their aeroplanes and to no one place. Many pilots show a great sensitiveness about the destruction of the German cities, which shows itself sometimes in aggressiveness, sometimes in a sense of shame. Such comments as, "Why, after all the trouble we've taken destroying German cities, are Mil. Gov. spoon-feeding the Germans?" are fairly typical. An Australian pilot whom I met extended his resentment to the Polish D.P.s. "They've had the cheek in one place to ask for a hot meal at midday—and to threaten a strike. They wouldn't have dreamed of striking against the Nazis." The women, of course, exaggerate the resentful attitudes of the R.A.F. On the other hand, one also hears doubts and regrets about our bombing policy. My general impression was that the R.A.F. are in a particularly unhappy position, because they are more concerned with what has been done than with any work which completely occupies them at present, unlike the Military Government which is entirely occupied with present problems. One has to make every allowance for the anxieties and the painful experiences of these men who have an extraordinary position in modern life: heroes who are required by our civilization to be heroic for a few years of their lives, after which they are expected to become bank clerks, etc.

After a week of concerts in the provinces, we went to Berlin. We were accompanied by a lady officer who was extremely nervous about the journey. 'She said that only the previous week two of her fellow officers, who had accidentally entered Berlin by way of Potsdam, had been held by the Russians for cross-questioning for two days. When we got near Berlin, there was a great rainstorm, and the whole of the dull, coarse, flat, grey-green Brandenburgian plain seemed merged into the streaming sky: and this sky seemed to reflect a mass of grey streaks like grass, wet lakes, and smeared views of pine forests. We left the main route because this was marked: "TO POTSDAM." After this all the signs were in Russian, which equally all seemed to lead to Potsdam. Our companion became more and more nervous and in the grey weather on the road which circles round Berlin we had the impression of being in an aeroplane circling above a 'drome in a pouring mist. I got out at a garage where I talked with some Germans who told me the way to Berlin without going through Potsdam. We had overshot the English Zone, passed through the Russian one, and come back into Berlin through the American Zone. At first Berlin seemed less damaged than I had expected, but as we approached the centre of the town, it produced the same impression of desolation as all the other large German towns.

How can one sum up this impression of desolation? It is as though a city were an organism which could survive when its heart has been destroyed. Life only continues at the edges of the German cities. The centre is broken and blackened, like the centre of a leaf which is brown and torn, although a vague green still surrounds the blackness and a few veins traverse it.

Berlin is—or was—a curiously planned city with centres separated from each other by railway systems, canals and the Spree. For example, there are two West Ends, the pompously Prussian Unter den Linden and the meretriciously dazzling Kurfürstendamm. These two entirely different conceptions of what a West End should be—whether a pretentious essay in studied Greek classicism or a Whore of Babylon—lie as it were in different bedrooms, like two mistresses of the Berlin soul, separated from each other by an immense network of railways spanned by a few enormous bridges. Now both false idols lie in ruins, and the bridges are nearly all down, so that to pass from one ruined centre of Berlin to another, one has to reconnoitre half a dozen temporary bridges and diversions.

The split between the two equally false West Ends was characteristic of the whole of Berlin. There was never a city which so lacked any quality of spontaneity. Everything about Berlin seemed strained and false, and at times, it plunged wildly into the fantastic. For example, the cathedral, the palace, and all the statues glorifying Prussian victories around it, the statues in the *Siegesallée* were comic or insane—as one liked to look at them. At the same time, they were expressions of aberrations of spirit which characterized the whole city. They could not be regarded as dilettantism, as æsthetic experimentation, or as individual eccentricity, like the Art nouveau of the Paris Metro or the unfinished cathedral at Barcelona of Gaudi.

For the contrasting spirits of Unter den Linden and of Kurfürstendamm had permeated the whole of Berlin. Even the stucco or the concrete-fronted tenements of the Hallesches Tor and the East End would break into a theme of battle-axes, cherubs and large-bosomed figures of Victory, while enormous stores or restaurants would swagger above the poorer streets in imitation of the gaudy brilliance of the Kurfürstendamm and the Wittenberg Platz.

When I lived in Berlin in 1930, I inhabited bed-sitting rooms. A search for a bed-sitting room in the neighbourhood of the Nollendorfplatz (near the Kurfürstendamm West End) in 1930 gave one some glimpses into the interior of houses which showed how macabre were the variations on the Prussian style. I shall never forget the heaviness of Berlin porticoes, the massiveness of the entrance halls, the insistence even in the design of a stove in a room on a style which seeks an alibi from the charge of pretentiousness in massiveness. One room which I was offered for the price of about one pound a week (with breakfast) was designed in a mixture of baronial and Gothic styles, being inlaid entirely with carved cedarwood; which gave it the smell and the air of the interior of a large cigar box. On a platform at one end of this room there stood the figures of four knights, in shining armour.

Of course, there is something profoundly disturbing in looking for rooms in any large city. It gives one a sensation very similar to that of reading a volume of horrific stories by Edgar Allan Poe. For Poe grasped that the idea of ghosts is inextricably bound up with style, fashion, architecture and the furniture of a room in an outmoded taste.

In parts of Berlin, such as Charlottenburg and Wilmersdorf, the architecture terrified me by the monotonous repetition of extravagant mouldings all emphasizing the same crude conceptions of war and fertility. Nothing has ever given me such a sensation of loneliness, bareness and anxiety, as some long Berlin street of grey houses, covered from top to bottom with carvings and figures, all of them the same on each house. Then perhaps at the end of the street, or in a gap between houses, or in a square, beyond which the street continued in a dead straight line, exactly the same as before, there would be some great ornamental building, with its lions and its tower, or equally aggressive in its modern plainness, which seemed the last word in emptiness and desolation.

Yet I liked Berlin. There were even things about the city which charmed me, for example the Tiergarten, and above all the Grunewald, where I used to go nearly every afternoon with Christopher Isherwood for a walk. It was my great admiration for Isherwood, the endless entertainment of his conversation and of his self-dramatization which kept me in Berlin, and which even got me in a state of mind in which I scarcely asked myself whether I wished to be anywhere else. And when at last he showed signs of growing tired of my admiring company, I left and never went back to live there again.

Yet there were other reasons why I liked Berlin. At this stage in my life Berlin seemed "realer" to me than any other city. To me it was the *reductio ad absurdum* of the contemporary situation, and I felt an inner necessity to grasp within myself the threadbare realities of the time in which I lived, before I could taste of the deeper traditions of France and Italy, and of the tragedy of Spain. All my experiences at Berlin were of a very "contemporary" kind. Berlin was a town where tradition was a caricature and a mockery, where action was conceived of entirely in terms of power—enormous power for good or for evil. Nor do I think that the possibility of good was by any means excluded. The vastness of the evil produced by Germany so overwhelms us to-day that it is difficult to maintain that there was also in Germany after the last war a great potentiality for good. Yet I believe that this is so: that thousands of people who supported what they called a "New Germany" of the Weimar Republic and of Social Democracy, were inspired by a great hope and a happy readiness to sacrifice their own interests for a good cause as much as they did later on for a bad one.

In this city without style, without tradition, one was conscious above all of everyone's sense that he or she was living in every way from day to day around a kind of zero. The strength and the weakness of the Berliners was their feeling that they could begin a completely new kind of life—because they had nothing to begin from. And when the New Life, the New Germany of the immediate post-war years experienced difficulties, they had the sensation that they had got back to nothing. It was this fatal feeling that if one way failed, then they were back at their starting point of zero (symbolized readily by the inflation), that there was no increment of tradition or idealism worth fighting for, which put many Germans who were not Nazis at the mercy of the Nazis. In 1932, I heard with a sinking heart and a sense of foreboding two remarks which illustrated this sense that a failure had brought them back to zero. One was from a well-known doctrinaire Marxist: "We must endure a Nazi régime for seven years, in order that it may produce a catastrophe from which Germany can only be saved by a Socialist Revolution." The other remark which one heard often in Berlin during the time of Brüning's government by Emergency Decree, was: "Things can't be worse than they are now. So we might as well try Hitler." The post-war Germans suffered from an inability to appreciate the truth of Edgar's observation in *King Lear:*

> And worst I may be yet: the worst is not
> So long as we can say "This is the worst."

With him also, they may now be reflecting:

> O gods! Who is't can say, "I am at the worst"?
> I am worse than e'er I was.

We stayed at the visitors' hotel, the Savoy, situated between the Berlin Zoological Gardens and the Kurfürstendamm. After dinner I went out alone and walked down the Kurfürstendamm along the Tauentzienstrasse, as far as the Wittenbergplatz. I wanted to recapture something of the mood of the Berlin I knew. The Gedaechtniskirche forms an island amid cross roads. On one side of it there was a café called the Café am Zoo where I often used to write while eating a fruit salad or drinking coffee, and beyond it there was the famous Romanisches Café which had the reputation of being the meeting place of Berlin's artistic and literary Bohemia. Hitler particularly hated this café and its inhabitants, and heaven knows to what ends of the earth and the universe its somewhat affected inhabitants, with their parade of ideas and small vices, were now scattered. On the left-hand side of the Tauentzienstrasse, there had been a very smart bar and restaurant—too smart for me—which was guarded at alternate hours of the day and night by one of two extremely handsome page boys, dressed in a green uniform. On the opposite side of the Tauentzienstrasse along roads leading off from it, there was a night club called *Femina* and one or two other haunts of vice. These places were no more vicious than other such places in other cities all over the world, but they were more notorious because there was nothing secret about them. They were open to every passer-by and many visitors to Berlin visited them in all their brazenness. One of the contributions of Germany to the rest of civilization ever since the time of Tacitus has been to make it feel virtuous in comparison with the Germans. Even the foreign correspondents living in Berlin were able to astonish themselves with their own purity by an occasional visit to one of Berlin's bars followed by an indignant article exporting something of its wicked glamour to their readers.

But the whole of this settled, elaborated life where the roads were like polished grooves and rails along which everyone who moved knew his or her destination, whether for good or for bad, had gone. The contours which I saw through the darkness were torn, ragged edges, the only noises which one heard were creakings and flappings, the two or three people who still haunted the streets were some American soldiers making their way to the bar in the Kurfürstendamm, where out of politeness one buys a drink but out of self-regard one does not drink it. The ruins of the Gedaechtniskirche—in its heyday the most hideous church outside Maida Vale—had now the enormous dignity of bare arches and shattered columns which perhaps makes the ruins of every civilization have a certain grandeur. I did not go very far. By the time I reached the Wittenbergplatz, with the vast skeleton of Kadewe—the Berlin Selfridges—on my right, I realized that everything was like this, that an enormous shroud of sameness had blurred and covered the whole face of Berlin and that nothing which I knew existed any longer.

The next morning I went the same walk by daylight. The Tauentzienstrasse seemed a frontage of grey cliffs of stone, torn and scratched and partly pulled down by winds and tides. All the city lay broken and exposed to the weather, and the few shops that had things to sell, the few tenements still inhabited had the small helplessness of hovels amid the surrounding disaster.

My wife and I visited the mother of a refugee friend. Another woman opened the door to us, and when we made inquiries for Frau —— she at first denied all knowledge of her. Then she said that she had gone away to the country. It took us about half an hour to convince her that we had come for no reason except to bring messages and a few small gifts. We arranged to call at a later hour when Frau —— had returned to her home. When we met her later, she seemed so tired and old that we hardly asked her about her experiences in Berlin, of which she did not complain. We thought it better to talk to her about her son.

Later, we made our way across the ruins of the city, to see those sights which are a very recent experience in our civilization, though they have characterized other civilizations in decay: ruins, not belonging to a past civilization, but the ruins of our own epoch, which make us suddenly feel that we are entering upon the nomadic stage when people walk across deserts of centuries, and when the environment which past generations have created for us disintegrates in our own lifetimes. The Reichstag and the Chancellory are already sights for sightseers, as they might well be in another five hundred years. They are the scenes of a collapse so complete that it already has the remoteness of all final disasters which make a dramatic and ghostly impression whilst at the same time withdrawing their secrets and leaving everything to the imagination. The last days of Berlin are as much matters for speculation as the last days of an empire in some remote epoch: and one goes to the ruins with the same sense of wonder, the same straining of the imagination, as one goes to the Colosseum at Rome.

The Reichstag is a vast shell, a central dome with passages and domes round it, charred inside and out, and covered from plinths to ceilings with the scrawling, unfamiliar Russian handwriting of the soldiers who triumphantly occupied it. The invaders still stroll round it staring, and stand round in the street outside. Like all the vaster ruins of Germany (Cologne Cathedral, for example) it has become a centre of black market, and people come up to you offering to sell you cameras, films and so on, in exchange for cigarettes. Then a race of Guides has also sprung up, people willing to show you where Hitler stood, and contemptuously repeat what he said. The building is a ruin, all the life organized round it has been cancelled overnight, and now everything is strange, as though the domes of this building were filled a few months ago not just with voices and with men but with a language and a way of thought which has now become only a matter of rumours and incredulity.

With the Chancellory the impression is more precise than with the Reichstag. For whereas the Reichstag is the shell of a theatre whose stage and scenery and actors have been destroyed and forgotten, the Chancellory is still full of clues, and almost of footmarks. Everything about it emphasized collapse and bewilderment. There were rooms still knee-deep in papers, though everything of significance had been taken and these reams of paper still left were mostly forms of various kinds or parts of unused filing systems. The policemen who guarded the Chancellory—who were members of the same force as had protected the Nazis—had now become showmen and touts. With grinning faces, they showed us the quarters occupied by Goebbels's family and Hitler's main reception room, with a few chairs in it from which all the stuffing had been ripped. The skeleton of a Venetian glass candelabra, from which the glass beads had been stolen, had been torn from the ceiling and reached, still hanging on one wire, to the floor. A long wooden table of very fine wood, an another table inlaid with rare stones, still survived. Outside the windows of this room, Hitler's desk, with a massive marble top, had been flung into the garden. Charwomen responsible for the upkeep of the Chancellory and still performing their tasks, concealed on their persons hammers with which they broke off fragments of the yellow marble top of this desk as souvenirs in exchange for a few cigarettes. The policemen furtively offered us Iron Crosses, Maternity Medals, or Good Conduct Medals, for five, three and two cigarettes respectively.

In its derelict condition, the main glory of the Chancellory seems to have consisted in its acres of tomato-coloured marble. Along the side of it there was a very long and wide and high corridor, with tall windows looking out onto a courtyard, in which there were a few burned-out tanks.

We were taken out of the main building across the garden to Hitler's shelter. The garden was a waste of mud and clay, filled with small fragments of broken glass, bombs, pottery, marble, etc., just as the plain of Mycenae, near Agamemnon's tomb, is covered with small fragments of pottery 2500 years old. The shelter itself was a rather elaborate, but by no means grandiose dug-out, containing, below, several rooms divided into two suites: one for Hitler and Eva Braun and one for the Goebbels family. Above Hitler's bed there were still many shelves of books on architecture. Hitler had spent the last months of his life resuming his architectural studies.

As we went away, I was thinking that the psychological clue to Nazism itself and to the hold which it had over its followers may well lie in the fact that Hitler before, as it were, he became Hitler, was the student of architecture who failed to pass the examinations which would have enabled him to study architecture at the University of Vienna; and that Goebbels before, as it were, he became Goebbels, was the student at the University of Heidelberg who wrote a bad verse drama on the life of Christ. The architect who failed to build had turned the foundations of every city in Germany to sand. The prophet who could not understand God had become the Satanic agent in a society where so far Satanism had ruled only in some pages of Baudelaire and of Dostoievsky.

These were not just tyrants who appeared for a time and then disappeared leaving a great deal of material destruction and physical suffering behind them—destruction which can be repaired, leaving its authors as a memory only. What they destroyed, once and for all, is the modern middle-class idea that man, as a social being, does not have to choose between good and evil. They involved almost the whole of the German middle classes—and a great section of the middle classes of Europe and the rest of the world in physical and moral damnation by forcing them to be really wicked and to be involved in wholly sinful actions. The world is now aghast with the realization that society has got to choose not just to be free but to be good.

If we are truthful with ourselves, we have to admit, surely, that political freedom has been tolerable and welcome to us, because we did not think that it confronted us with direct responsibility of a choice between good and evil. We were free because we believe in "laissez-faire," in the old-fashioned conception of evolution, in the sense of having confidence that an interplay of free forces and conflicting interests would inevitably produce the best results. And no one was responsible for these results, no one was responsible for progress. If one was a reformer or even a radical revolutionary, one was still only a force within a total of conflicting forces which were producing the general movement of social advancement, so that in a sense it was true that the people who were opposed to reform, the conservatives, were contributing as much to the general progress (in that they themselves represented one of the forces of society), as the progressives.

Freedom thus meant freedom within a general framework outside the individual's control, to express one's own individuality. The automatism of society coupled with the conception of indivual freedom, puzzled and disturbed the minds of the greatest thinkers of the nineteenth century. In a sense they were depressed by this freedom which at the same time robbed them of the power of complete moral action within the society in which they lived. On the other hand, that depression seemed selfish so long as one accepted the idea that the laissez-faire automatism of society was genuinely progressive. Thus both the social optimism and the social pessimism of the poets of the nineteenth century are unconvincing, wilful and open to the criticism that they are subjective. For since progress is an automatism outside anyone's control, or even the control of any group, one cannot identify oneself with the whole of progressive society, as, say, one can identify oneself with a Church or with the French Revolution. One can only identify oneself with some partial movement within it. This, indeed, is what the most convincing writers of the period do: Dickens, for example, in general gives the impression of being an optimist, on the side of Progress, but at the same time he identifies himself passionately with causes which are real forces within the general automatism of Progress, such as penal reform.

However, the gloom of Tennyson, the ennui of Baudelaire and the pessimism of Thomas Hardy, lay these writers open to the charge of subjectivism. Fundamentally they are asking the progressive age to provide them with human solace, with a meaning in life, which it is not the business of such a society to provide. Society is there, the business men and the progressives agree, to provide an increasing number of people with increasing material benefits for increasing material demands. If man requires spiritual consolations and other kinds of significance, he may look elsewhere, perhaps to the poets. Why do the poets complain that society does not give them something which they should be giving to society? It is the business of the poets to manufacture Beauty, and perhaps Faith, in the same way as it is the business of Henry Ford to manufacture motor cars.

The poets reply by saying that modern society does not make man happy. In the nineteenth century it was certainly arguable that this was a one-sided and subjective judgment. The ennui of Baudelaire, the black moods of Tennyson, the pessimism of Hardy, the morbidity of Dostoievsky, were discounted as invalid criticism of life, as subjective judgments. (Doubtless the uncertain margin between the subjective and the social judgments in modern literature accounts for and justifies the great curiosity to-day in the biographies of artists: people want to find out whether it is the fault of society or of the artists themselves that the artists were unhappy.)

That the Nazist and the Fascist leaders were often disappointed artists is deeply significant. Goebbels's intuition that the Nazis were doing in political life what Dostoievsky could only do in literature is profound. However cheap, however base, however cynical the Nazis were, they did succeed in being something which the laissez-faire age never responsibly was; that is to say, really wicked. They made social and political activity significant moral, or rather immoral, activity, and they renounced the irresponsible amoral automatism of the progressive industrial era. As human beings, they were at the centre of their own social actions and in a universe which, if it does not include the idea of heaven, at least includes the idea of hell, they damned and destroyed themselves and a great part of the world with them. In them, Satan was incarnated, and the pieces of Hitler's desk which I carried away with me had a significance which makes them unholy relics in exactly the same way as other relics are holy.

Thus can I explain to myself why it is that these terrible men preoccupied (I can witness only for myself) not only my waking thoughts but also my dreams, during many years. And in my dreams, I did not simply hate them and put them from me. I argued with them, I wrestled with their spirits, and the scene in which I knew them was one in which my own blood and tears flowed. The cities and soil of Germany where they were sacrificed were not just places of material destruction. They were altars on which a solemn sacrifice had been performed according to a ritual in which inevitably all the nations took part. The whole world had seemed to be darkened with their darkness, and when they left the world, the threat of a still greater darkness, a total and everlasting one, rose up from their ashes. And at the same time, there could not be the least doubt that the only answer to this past and this present is a conscious, deliberate and wholly responsible determination to make our society walk in paths of light.

26th March 1946.